Serving
Maps
on the
Internet

geographic information
on the world wide web

Christian Harder

Published by
Environmental Systems Research Institute, Inc.
380 New York Street
Redlands, California 92373-8100

Environmental Systems Research Institute, Inc.
Serving Maps on the Internet: Geographic Information on the World Wide Web
ISBN 1-879102-52-8

Contents

Preface

Systems for managing information according to geography are, in one sense, as old as the earliest maps. Only recently, however, with computer technology, have we been able to manage vast quantities of information with speed and flexibility.

Today, almost everything that moves or changes over time is being measured and converted into digital information, enabling us to organize our activities and our environment at unprecedented levels of detail and accuracy.

The rate of change in less than twenty years has been phenomenal. In the early 1980s, there were several hundred people using geographic information systems, or GIS. Today there are at least a quarter of a million, and by early in the next century there will be tens of millions.

This is partly because of simultaneous improvements in computing power, databases, measuring technologies, and GIS software. But the change has become exponential largely because of networking technologies, the Internet in particular.

What's emerging is something I call *societal GIS*, an electronic web of geographic information that anyone can access. Even people without computers can go to a library and make use of a vast array of databases from around the globe.

Serving Maps on the Internet presents case studies of a dozen different private and public organizations that are delivering geographic information. Each case study shows how these organizations have extended their activities into the community and realized enormous and often unexpected benefits by openly sharing their data.

Jack Dangermond
Founder and president
ESRI

Acknowledgments

This book could not have been written without the cooperation of the organizations that shared their applications and reviewed the material for accuracy. You'll find the individuals from those organizations acknowledged by name at the end of each case study.

A number of people at ESRI also contributed time and expertise.

In the early stages of development, Sandi Peterson, Bob Ruschman, Diane Shimota, Deane Kensock, Jim McKinney, Charlie Barnwell, and Eric Culp all helped identify case-study candidates.

Michael Karman and Tim Ormsby edited numerous versions of the manuscript and made contributions to the text. Michael Hyatt designed the book, laid out and produced the pages, and did the copyediting and proofreading. Gina Davidson designed and produced the cover, and Cliff Crabbe oversaw print production.

Mike Tait, Art Haddad, Ming Zhao, and David Maguire of ESRI, along with Dr. Michael Shiffer of the Massachusetts Institute of Technology, provided technical information and reviewed the final manuscript. Peter C. Schreiber, Esq., and Barbara Shaeffer of ESRI also reviewed the manuscript.

Clem Henricksen, Rick Schneblin, Erin Pearse, and the ArcExplorer Team were largely responsible for creating the content on the companion CD–ROM.

Kate Anger offered sage advice and moral support.

Judy Boyd provided technical and human resources and Bill Miller set high standards for quality design. Finally, special thanks to Jack Dangermond, who wrote the preface and also recognized the value of book publishing at ESRI.

Chapter 1

Internet mapping: Serving geographic data on the Web

The convergence of geographic information systems (GIS) and the World Wide Web has changed mapmaking forever. Once painstakingly produced by mechanical means, detailed maps can now be generated on demand from huge databases of spatial information and transmitted instantly across the globe. Suddenly GIS, until recently a specialized tool of scientists and city planners, is dispensing all manner of geographic information to an enthusiastic Internet audience.

Internet GIS

The Internet doesn't change the fundamental nature of GIS, it just gets it online. But that's comparable to saying that a printing press doesn't change the fundamental nature of a book. The value of geographic information (like all forms of digital information) and the power of GIS applications to solve problems are proportional to their accessibility.

Every day, millions of people access geographic information via the Internet. Most of them, like the commuter who checks freeway conditions, the last-minute shopper looking for the nearest candy store, or the executive who needs directions to a business meeting, probably don't realize they're using a geographic information system.

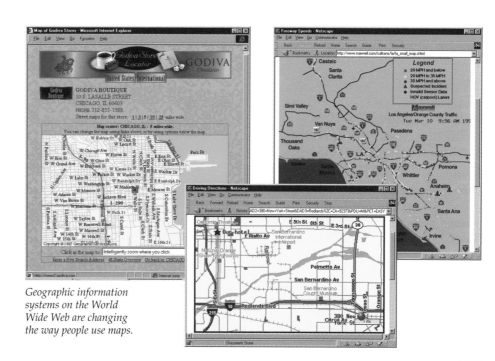

Geographic information systems on the World Wide Web are changing the way people use maps.

What's possible with Internet GIS?

So what are some of the things that can and will be done with this technology? The most common applications are location services like the chapter locator on the Service Corps of Retired Executives (SCORE) Web site developed by Geographic Services Corp. Typing an address or street intersection into a simple form gets the Web user a map of the nearest SCORE chapter.

Routing and direction services are also becoming wildly popular. The zip2.com Web site offers point-to-point routing for any address in the United States. Similar services are coming online for other parts of the world as companies develop the highly accurate digital street databases required.

Even the age-old atlas has gone electronic. The *ArcAtlas™: Our Earth* digital atlas from ESRI includes finished maps, interactive maps, and multimedia content linked to points on the maps.

Some map-based Web sites exist just to notify people about things like road construction in their neighborhood, or the shipment routes of nuclear waste in America.

Location services

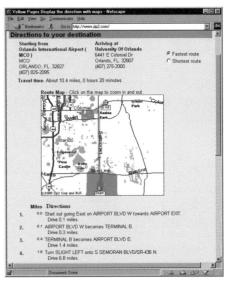

Routing and direction services

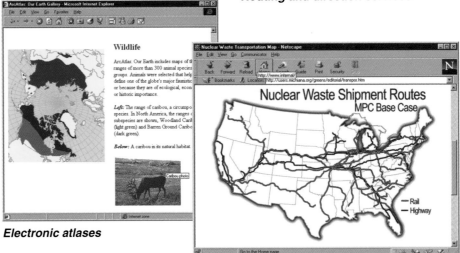

Electronic atlases

Public notification

Many public agencies are opening their databases to the public. The City of Ontario, California, has set up an application that allows people to query the city's parcel tax database for a specific owner or tax ID number and get a map of the parcel along with a detailed tax history of that subject.

The Berkeley Police Department's Interactive Crime Maps Web page allows citizens to see various crime patterns (like murder) in relation to other crime patterns (like auto theft) and to where they live.

Other Internet-based geographic information systems map demographics. One sophisticated new program is the CIESIN® Java™-based Demographic Data Viewer, a research tool that provides rapid access to census data coupled with a fast and powerful mapping application.

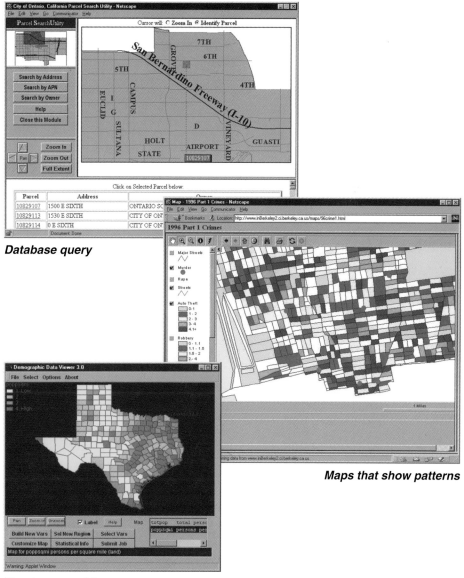

Database query

Maps that show patterns

Geodemographic maps

Measuring technologies (known as remote sensing in GIS circles) now track and record an incredible variety of natural and human phenomena. These measurements result in useful databases, like the real-time Southern California traffic maps that retrieve data from roadway sensors and show actual traffic speed on a Web page. Not a bad thing for a commuter to check before hopping onto the freeway for the drive home (or not, if too many red dots line the route).

Another by-product of the wealth of available earth data are maps that display environmental conditions. Like the map of fault lines in Southern California's desert seen on this page, these maps have great value to people who live, work, and build homes in a particular region.

As Internet capacity increases and computers become more powerful, more and more sites will offer specialized GIS service. People will come to these sites looking for an answer to a question, such as "Show me the route to Chicago that passes the most national parks, then give me a list of kid-friendly hotels in Chicago."

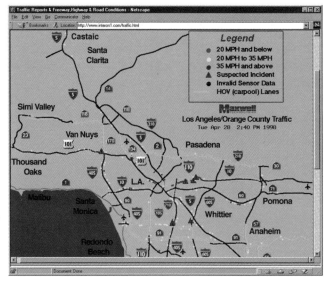

Changing phenomena

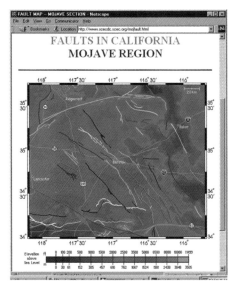

Environmental condition maps

The many faces of Internet GIS

Geographic information on the Web ranges from maps that are created for you, which you read as you would a paper map, all the way to sophisticated applications that you use to build complex queries like "show me all the vacant corner properties that face streets that see at least thirty cars a minute going in each direction" or "make me a route from my hotel to the convention center that takes in as many sights as possible in a thirty-minute drive."

Maps that only show location

Simplest in terms of technology are the Web sites that present the digital equivalent of paper maps, such as the map of Marina del Rey (an affluent beachfront section of Los Angeles) found on the Ritz Carlton Hotel chain's Web site. Because the location of the hotel is unlikely to change anytime soon, a permanent map is all that's needed to help guests plan their trips.

Maps such as these are often digitally scanned from a paper map, though they can also be drawn with a CAD program or created with a desktop-mapping program like ESRI's ArcView® GIS software. The final maps are then saved as standard GIF or JPEG image files and served on the Web embedded in standard HTML documents.

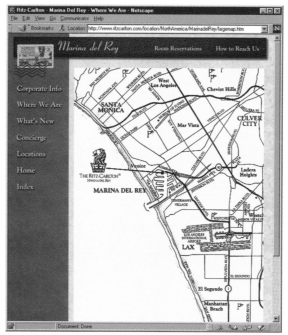

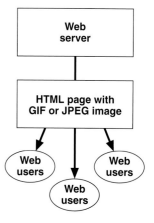

Maps like this, while not interactive, do contribute to distributing geographic information on the Web.

Maps that show change

Geographic information that changes over time (like weather patterns) can be shown with frequently updated maps. The example on this page, from the Weather Channel's Web site, is a satellite weather map, replaced hourly with a fresh image beamed down from low earth orbit. Many types of GIS data—like traffic volumes or earthquake frequencies—also lend themselves to this type of presentation.

From a technical standpoint, the maps are served just like the hotel map on the preceding page—as an embedded GIF or JPEG image. The difference is that a script running in the background replaces the image whenever a new one becomes available.

The application seen here can also provide recent historical information by allowing the user to play back a string of images from the last few hours to create an animated weather movie.

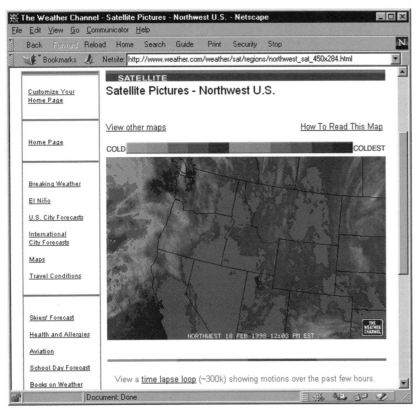

Each hour the image at this site is replaced with a newer one.

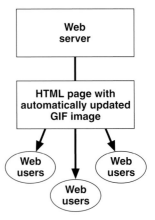

Maps that the user creates

Much of the emphasis on the Internet these days is on delivering interactive content that users can manipulate. GIS provides the ability to generate maps "on the fly" according to specific queries entered by the user.

With the Massachusetts Electronic Atlas, for example, the user selects the data and controls the geographic area to be displayed (from statewide down to the town level). The map is updated or re-created each time a new request is sent to the

server. While the example shown displays just one variable (median household income), the entire database contains hundreds of variables that can be mapped in thousands of different combinations.

Users send instructions about maps they want to see by submitting requests to the Web server. Using the TCP/IP protocol, the server connects to ArcView Internet Map Server, which renders the map and returns it as a GIF or JPEG image embedded in an HTML document or Java application.

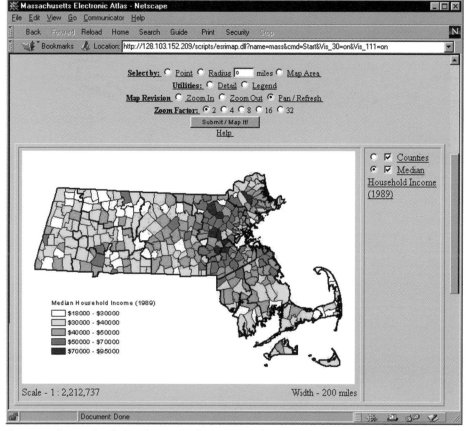

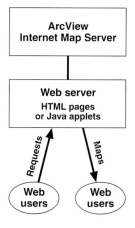

A new map is created each time the user sends a request to the system.

Maps that perform spatial analysis

In mapping applications that perform spatial analysis, users not only generate a map based on a specific request and set of data, they also direct the system to analyze geographic relationships. Common relationships include distance (for instance, from the airport to the hotel), containment (the number of medium-priced restaurants within 1 mile of the office), and networking (the quickest route from the convention center to the beach).

The dealer locator example shown on this page was developed for a lawnmower manufacturer. When you want to locate the dealer nearest your home, you are prompted for details about the product you want and, most importantly, for your home address.

In this example, the raw map data is stored in ESRI's Spatial Database Engine™ (SDE™) spatial data access engine in order to handle large databases and turn around spatial queries quickly. Like the example on the preceding page, users communicate with the system by sending requests to the server, which then returns a map and results to the user.

The system locates the three nearest dealers based on driving time (the geographic analysis) and generates a map showing the location of your home and the selected dealers.

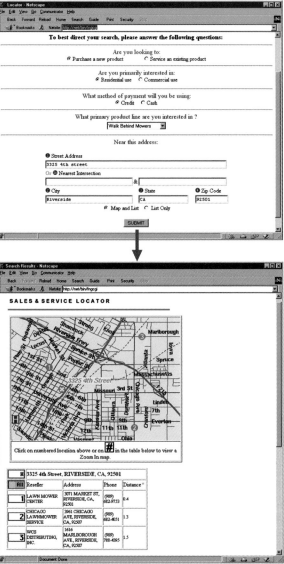

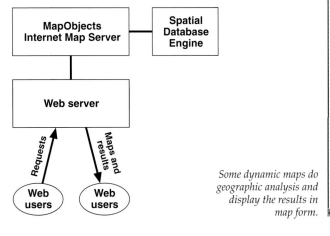

Some dynamic maps do geographic analysis and display the results in map form.

Maps that perform geoprocessing

Yet another form of Internet mapping application is one that processes the geographic data or transforms it, like this hillshade image generator from the West Virginia Environmental Protection Agency.

Hillshading simulates the effect of sunlight on the earth's surface. By selecting a map quadrangle and a sun position (specified in terms of azimuth and angle above horizon), the user can generate and display an image of terrain in relief.

Because there are tens of millions of possible combinations of quadrangle and sun position, it would be impractical to store all these images on the server. Instead, the selections are passed to a GIS image analysis program (in this case, ESRI's ARC/INFO® software), which performs the analysis on the raw data and returns the rendered image. Because the image analysis takes place on a powerful UNIX® server, the work is done in a second or two and can be performed simultaneously for many concurrent users.

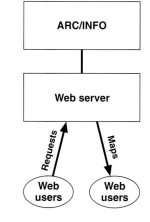

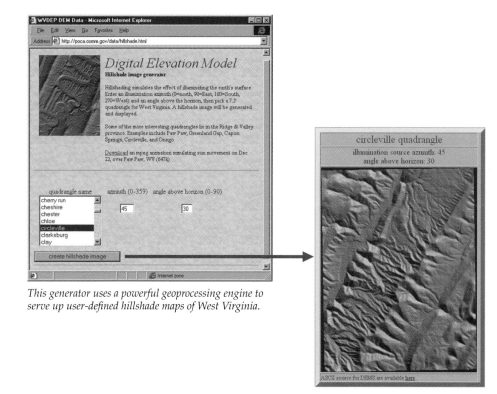

This generator uses a powerful geoprocessing engine to serve up user-defined hillshade maps of West Virginia.

Public data sites

As geographic information systems have become widespread over the past few years, a massive amount of geographically referenced data has been placed on the Internet. These spatial data libraries are part of the Web GIS story for two reasons: they are accessed through cartographic interfaces, and their contents are used to run many GIS applications.

In appendix B, you'll find some resources for locating the data you need to spatially enable your own Web site.

Spatial data sites like those seen on this page generally work as follows: you browse the available data and select the variables and geography needed. The request is processed and the actual GIS data (not a picture of a map) is downloaded to you, so you can see the data and manipulate it using your own GIS or desktop-mapping programs.

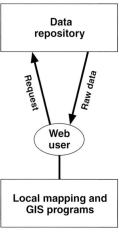

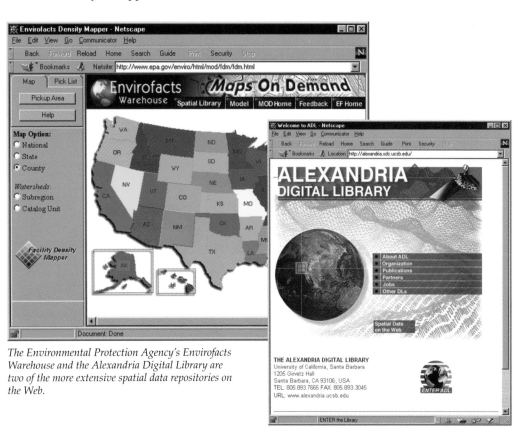

The Environmental Protection Agency's Envirofacts Warehouse and the Alexandria Digital Library are two of the more extensive spatial data repositories on the Web.

Commercial data sites

Related to the free data repositories seen on the preceding page are the commercial data vendor sites, like this one located at www.stickmap.com. This application uses a map-based interface to allow users to search the company's inventory of specialized oil exploration data. The red areas seen on the Texas map are actually comprised of many individual "seismic lines" that indicate the likelihood of oil reserves.

As more and more companies come to realize that their spatial data may be of use to others, vendor sites like this one will proliferate.

Technically, commercial sites work much like the public data sites: they deliver raw data to the user who can use it directly. The difference is that a transaction server is also in place to facilitate an electronic payment.

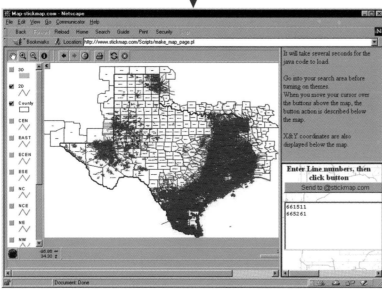

The Internet is becoming an active marketplace for many products. Spatial data vendors use map-based interfaces to sell data.

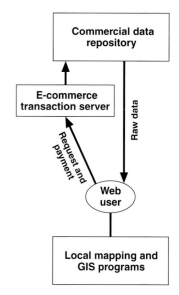

Internet GIS technology

In the remainder of this chapter, you'll learn a bit about the history of Web-based GIS technology, how the current Internet supports mapping, and about the future direction of Internet mapping.

Web GIS history

The technology used to deliver interactive mapping applications to the Internet has come a long way in the five years since the Xerox® Palo Alto Research Center (PARC) put up the first Web page with an active map as an experiment in interactive information retrieval.

As the first Internet mapping site, the developers had no easy way to provide the needed functionality. There were no forms and no Internet-specific programming languages like Java. The page was pure HTML, with a series of links for selecting options such as Zoom In, Show Rivers, and so on. Every possible option was written as a separate HTML page, and each choice linked the user to the appropriate page.

The Xerox PARC Map Viewer was discontinued in 1997 after four years of service, but not before showing the way for the thousands of map servers to come.

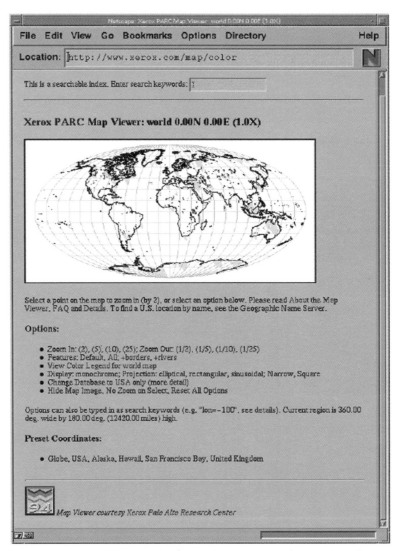

The Xerox PARC Map Viewer (now defunct) is widely recognized as the Internet's first interactive map server.

Client/Server 101

While this book is not a primer on setting up map-based Web applications, it's impossible to talk about the technology in even the most general terms without some background on how the Internet, and specifically the World Wide Web, actually works. Fortunately, at the conceptual level, it's not that complicated.

It's all about clients and servers. A client/server system consists of two programs that communicate across a computer network following an established communication language called a *protocol*.

For the purposes of this book, the network is either the Internet or a secure closed network equivalent called an *intranet*. The protocol is called HTTP, for HyperText Transfer Protocol.

The most common client program is called a Web browser. Netscape Navigator® and Microsoft® Internet Explorer are the most popular commercial browsers. When a user types a specific Web address, called a URL (Uniform Resource Locator), into the Web browser, the browser program sends a request to the server computer located at that address. (An Internet address is a name or number that uniquely identifies a computer in the universe of computers, just as a mailing address uniquely identifies a house in the universe of houses.) The server program then loads a file from its disk and transmits it over the Internet to the client browser.

On the server side, there are often many technologies working together to provide an increasingly sophisticated blend of information and services. In the context of map-based systems, it's useful to think of the server side as consisting of databases and middleware technology. The databases are where the actual data is stored in raw form. The middleware tier includes the technologies like CGI, DCOM, and CORBA that break the information into small chunks (called packets) and check that the packets were received by the client computer on the other side of the transaction.

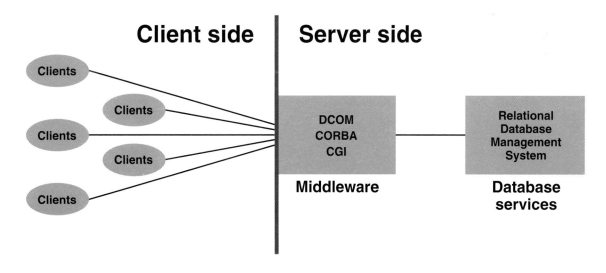

Client side | **Server side**

Clients

Clients

Clients

Clients

Clients

DCOM
CORBA
CGI

Middleware

Relational
Database
Management
System

**Database
services**

Object orientation

Driving many of the developments in software programming these days is the notion of object-oriented technology. Objects are self-contained, reusable software components that are combined to create complete applications. For GIS application developers, object-oriented technology cleaves huge chunks of time from project timetables because it allows them to reuse code and objects and to create new objects from existing ones. Objects are developed according to emerging component standards (like the Microsoft COM architecture) that enable them to work together across networks, hardware, and operating systems. The availability of GIS component software has made possible the networked GIS.

Networked GIS

The Internet is a global, public collection of computer networks. The term *intranet* describes a private network that operates on Internet standards, or protocols. The unifying protocol is the Internet Protocol (IP) that allows heterogeneous hardware to communicate effectively.

In a networked environment, basic GIS functionality in the form of objects is transmitted over the Internet (or intranet) and executed individually. Networked GIS solves the bandwidth problem by assigning the actual geoprocessing—the "heavy lifting"—to the local computer. And as the geoprocessing objects evolve they will deliver increasingly powerful functionality that any computer user can access.

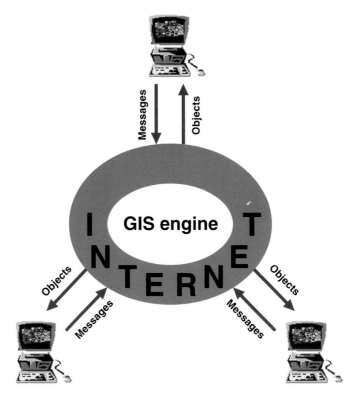

Where it's all heading

Because of the obvious synergy created by connecting GIS to the Internet, much research is now being conducted into how these systems will evolve. The Computer Resource Laboratory (CRL) of the MIT Department of Urban Studies and Planning has a number of research projects in the works that hint at what's in store. The laboratory's work suggests that geographic information systems, multimedia representational aids, spatial data access tools, and urban modeling software will blend into one seamless computing environment that will have a significant influence on the way people think and communicate about urban and regional places.

To stimulate discussion of these issues, the CRL has placed links to a number of its projects online at gis.mit.edu/projects.

This interactive Web interface allows users to click on a node on a map to show a 360-degree, panoramic view of a place.

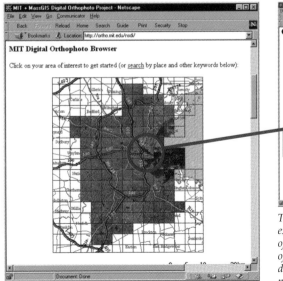

This application does on-the-fly extraction, formatting, and downloading of digital ortho photos from a repository of orthos that are cataloged and documented in accordance with metadata standards.

GIS in everyday life

Thanks to the successful marriage of geographic information systems and the Internet, we are finally within reach of organizing our knowledge of the earth and integrating that knowledge into our daily lives. GIS has become fast, easy to use, affordable, accessible, and broadly relevant. The age of societal GIS is upon us.

Societal GIS is a state in which geographic information is part of the framework of our conscious lives, and touches every aspect of daily existence.

More than ever before, we now use electronic geographic information systems to answer the fundamental questions that affect much of human endeavor: Where is it? and How do I get there?

As these systems evolve, people won't even think about it in terms of using a GIS. They'll just have a geospatial question or problem they want answered or solved.

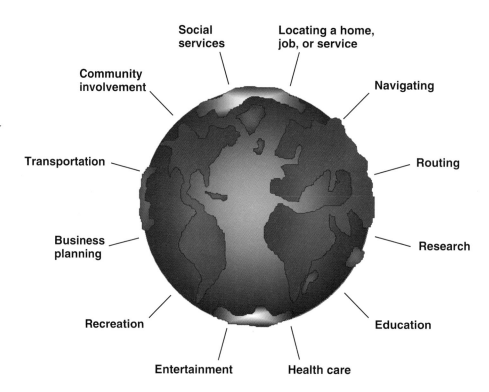

Social services

Locating a home, job, or service

Community involvement

Navigating

Transportation

Routing

Business planning

Research

Recreation

Education

Entertainment

Health care

The real world

In this book, you'll see how various organizations use GIS on the Web to serve their audiences.

Some technical information is provided, mostly to give a sense of the overall system architecture. This is not a how-to manual for using any of the software technology mentioned, nor is it a book about how to set up a Web site.

See appendix A, "The ESRI Internet mapping story," to learn what's involved in deploying simple mapping sites with ArcView Internet Map Server (IMS), or developing more sophisticated interactive GIS applications with MapObjects™ Internet Map Server.

Organizations like these are finding that Internet GIS represents an ideal way to communicate geographic information to a broad audience.

Chapter 2

•••• P u b l i c - a c c e s s   G I S

County government agencies in the United States maintain information about local lands (such as ownership, property values, and taxes due) that they are required to make publicly available. In most counties, if you need to know something about a specific parcel of land, you trek down to the county offices and ask a busy employee to look it up for you. Thanks to the Internet, however, that routine is beginning to change.

In this chapter, you'll see how one county government in North Carolina used the ESRI® MapObjects Internet Map Server to build a GIS application that allows people to access the county's complete land records database from any computer connected to the World Wide Web.

Cabarrus County

Incorporated in 1792, Cabarrus County originally gained notoriety as the place where gold was first discovered in the United States. After the gold rush ended, the rich "black jack" lands of western Cabarrus were found to be ideal for growing cotton. The textile mills came next, and, by 1840, Cabarrus was the nation's leading producer of cotton fabric. Textiles remain the dominant industry in Cabarrus County to this day.

These days, Cabarrus County is still noteworthy, but now it's for its innovative use of computer technology and its commitment to deploying government on the Web.

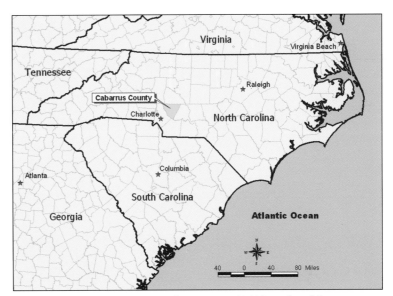

Cabarrus County, North Carolina, is home to over 100,000 people and the Charlotte Motor Speedway.

The spirit of e-gov

The government of Cabarrus County first launched its Web site (www.co.cabarrus. nc.us) in 1996, with the idea of making the more frequently requested public information available. Since people liked it, the government quickly developed a truly interactive site that allowed taxpayers to connect with their elected officials and tax-funded agencies.

This collection of Web-based services—dubbed e-gov—now includes things like the building code, information on the Board of Commissioners, parks and recreation schedules, employment opportunities, permit and inspection statistics, and a complete calendar of government meetings and events. The benefit of publishing this data on the Web has been enormous (and in some cases unexpected). For example, since the schedules have been published, fewer people call the main switchboard with routine questions, and more people come to public meetings. Attendance is up at local parks and recreation areas, too.

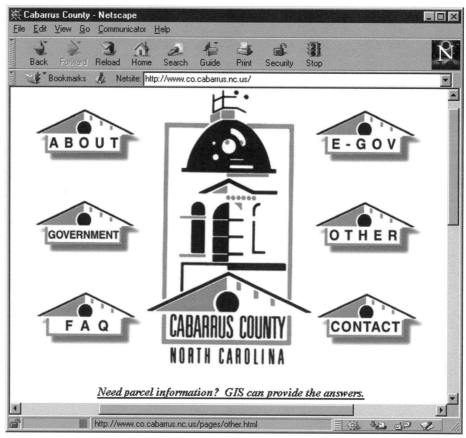

This is the home page of Cabarrus County, North Carolina. From here, people can access a wealth of important information, including a map-based parcel information locator.

Querying the parcel database

When the tax assessor's office wanted to publish its parcel tax database, the GIS department was called in to add a mapping component to the site.

The idea was that locals should have an easy way to access parcel and tax data, the sort of data frequently requested by property appraisers, real estate agents, and people involved in property disputes or tax challenges. The original plan called for a custom ArcView GIS application to run on workstations at the front counter of the land records division.

But when ESRI's MapObjects Internet Map Server was announced, the original plan was scrapped in favor of a purely Web-based application. The hope was that the same Web-based application could provide both internal access to government employees (through an intranet) and external access to all of Cabarrus County (and the world, as it turned out).

Created with Visual Basic® and MapObjects software, the simple interface allows either exact queries or general map searches. Users who know the exact address or parcel ID number can enter it and go directly to the map and table for that parcel, or they can use zoom and pan tools to locate parcels they may not have an address or ID number for.

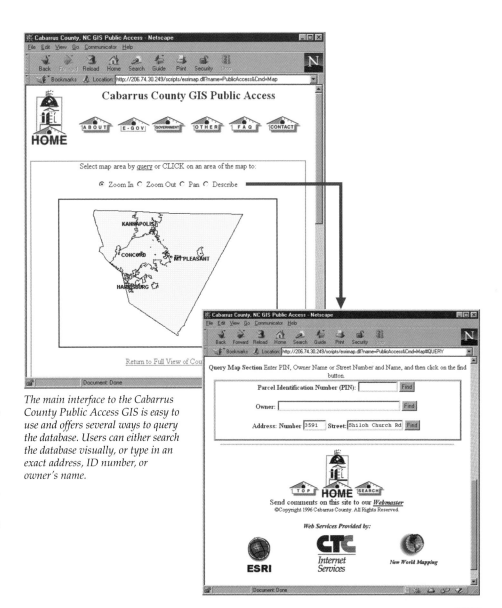

The main interface to the Cabarrus County Public Access GIS is easy to use and offers several ways to query the database. Users can either search the database visually, or type in an exact address, ID number, or owner's name.

Getting results

Once a unique parcel has been selected, the application displays a map of the immediate area, with the selected parcel outlined in green.

Choosing the Describe option and pointing to the parcel then brings up a complete table of information about the land in question, including owner's name, tax value, the last price the parcel was sold for, how it's zoned, what school district it's in, and so forth.

Real estate agents who used to visit the county offices to research a certain property (during government business hours) can now access the same information for as many properties as they want, twenty-four hours a day, seven days a week. Surprisingly, Web site statistics generated from the server reveal that many of the "hits" on the site come from outside Cabarrus County. While some of these hits originate in nearby Charlotte, a number also come from out of state and even overseas.

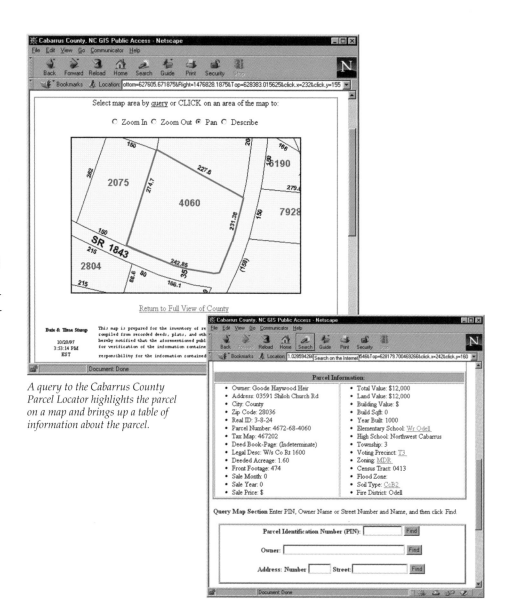

A query to the Cabarrus County Parcel Locator highlights the parcel on a map and brings up a table of information about the parcel.

The power of hyperlinks

Users get more than parcel information, too. That's because the architects of the Cabarrus County Public Access GIS project also exploited one of the fundamental strengths of the World Wide Web: the ability to connect or "hyperlink" to other sites.

Looking at the Parcel Information table, you see that certain items are underlined. Clicking on any of these words connects you to a different site. Clicking on a school name, for instance, links to a description of each school at the district's own Web server; clicking on the voting precinct brings up a map of the voting districts; clicking on the cryptic "CcB2" brings up a detailed description of soil makeup and ground slope, the wildlife found there, and the implications of building on that type of soil.

It's a mutually beneficial situation—the staff has more time for other things and the public can get answers to questions faster and without the inconvenience of a trip downtown.

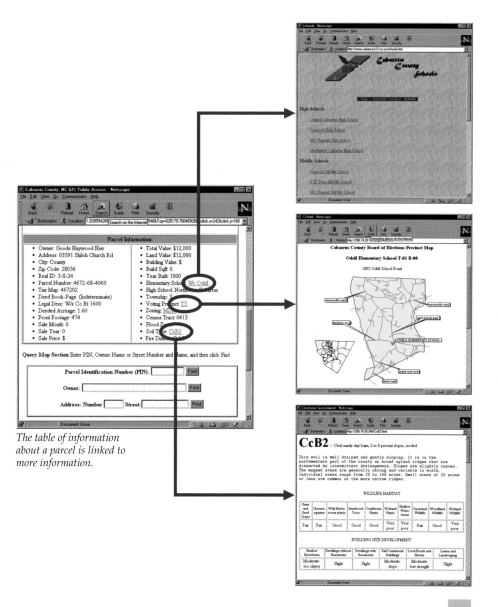

The table of information about a parcel is linked to more information.

Keeping the data current

Long before it deployed the Internet application, Cabarrus County was using a GIS database, much like many other local government agencies across the country.

With ARC/INFO software, ESRI's work-horse GIS, specialists from various county departments update unique map layers (or coverages) specific to their function. For example, the land records department updates the parcel boundaries layer, while the registrar of voters is responsible for keeping the voting district maps current.

Keeping the data current is crucial. Once a week, a COBOL program running on the county's IBM® ES/9000® mainframe computer retrieves the latest tax records

into a text file and transfers the data over a local network to the GIS department's Windows NT® workstation. GIS staff members then convert the tables from ASCII text to dBASE® for use with ArcView GIS software.

Next, a custom Avenue™ script pulls the parcel layers from an ARC/INFO library into ArcView GIS, joins the tax records table to the parcel layer, converts the data into shapefiles, adds some additional fields, and finally indexes key fields to speed up user-defined searches. The Avenue script automates these tasks, ensuring that the work is done the same way each week.

The data is saved directly onto the MapObjects Internet Map Server, ready for use. Once all the manipulations are complete, the Web application is halted, the data updated, and the application restarted.

In just a few hours, the data is current and complete, ready for the upwards of 2,500 times it will be accessed in the next week.

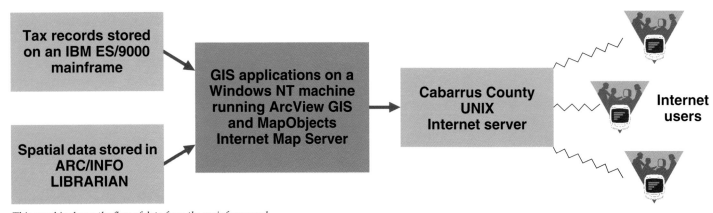

This graphic shows the flow of data from the mainframe and UNIX computers, where the source data is stored, to the GIS map server and finally out to the Internet-connected public.

Data

Highways and ZIP Codes included with ArcView GIS software.

Parcel and tax data from the Cabarrus County Assessor's Office.

Software

ArcView GIS

MapObjects Internet Map Server

ARC/INFO

ARC/INFO LIBRARIAN

Acknowledgments

Thanks to Suzanne Boyd and the entire GIS Department, Cabarrus County, North Carolina.

Chapter 3

• • • • • Disaster response networks

Earthquakes and other natural disasters can neither be prevented nor predicted with any great success. Since the utilities that deliver crucial public services like electricity, water, and communications are so vulnerable, major utility providers have developed comprehensive emergency response systems to monitor damage to their equipment and dispatch repair crews as quickly as possible.

In this chapter, you'll learn how a major electric utility in California developed an Internet application that gives its employees information about earthquakes almost before the ground stops shaking.

Power to the people

Southern California Edison, an Edison International company, is the nation's second largest investor-owned electric utility, serving more than eleven million customers in central, coastal, and southern California.

As electric utilities undergo the same sort of deregulation that transformed the phone companies a decade ago, SCE has turned its attention to applying technologies like GIS to help it perform better, and thereby compete more effectively.

SCE already relies on GIS technology to manage its day-to-day operations (through an established discipline known as Automated Mapping/Facilities Management, or AM/FM). What has changed in the new era is the number of ways that GIS is being applied.

While this familiar silhouette will remain part of the electric landscape, new technologies like GIS and the Internet are changing the way electric companies do business.

Team GIAS

SCEnet is the name of Southern California Edison's intranet. Authorized users on the SCEnet can access a special GIAS (Geographic Information Analysis Systems) home page with links to several live interactive GIS applications.

The application that's used the most is a tool for viewing and querying live maps of the entire SCE electric infrastructure. Since the data is downloaded automatically from the server each time it's accessed, engineers know that they're always working with the most current information, information that's used for important everyday tasks like load balancing, where technicians look for areas using more energy than usual so that they can guard against power interruptions.

The GIAS intranet page also includes links to other spatially enabled Web applications, such as a tool developed for a large retailer that monitors power consumption as it's happening and an application that allows SCE managers to assess the quality of service being delivered to their customers twenty-four hours a day, 365 days a year.

But perhaps the most interesting link on the page is the one that connects to SCE's emergency response network and the TriNet Project information system. The combined system allows access to utility data and links to other data resources.

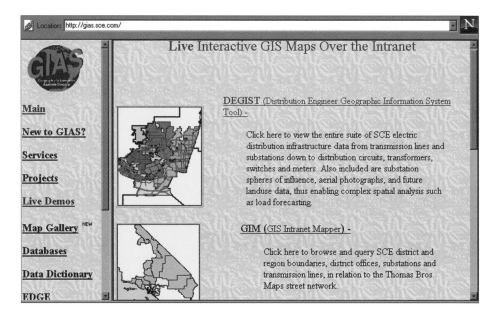

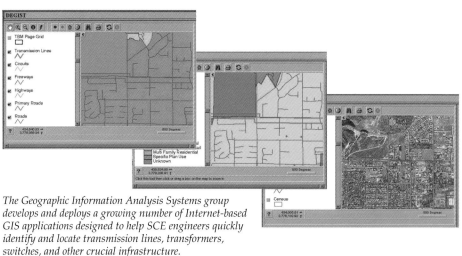

The Geographic Information Analysis Systems group develops and deploys a growing number of Internet-based GIS applications designed to help SCE engineers quickly identify and locate transmission lines, transformers, switches, and other crucial infrastructure.

The TriNet Project

The TriNet Project, sponsored by a unique alliance of public and private organizations, was created to reduce earthquake hazards by exploiting the latest advances in computer and telecommunications technologies.

The California Institute of Technology (Caltech), the U.S. Geological Survey, and the California Strong Motion Instrumentation Program have teamed with technology vendors to create an information system capable of providing real-time data on seismic activity to emergency response managers. Like the managers at SCE, these people can use this information when they need to shut down services; to protect communications lines; to stop air, highway, or rail traffic; and to inform the public about the extent of the crisis by getting news to the local media.

In the past, it could take SCE emergency response teams up to thirty minutes to learn the time, location, and magnitude of an earthquake. The TriNet Project will enable them to access this data while the ground is still shaking.

In the aftermath of a serious earthquake, time is of the essence. Above, these rescue crews in Santa Cruz, California, discuss strategy following the devastating 1989 Loma Prieta quake.

Enter EMIGA

For its own implementation of the TriNet system, SCE developed an application dubbed EMIGA, for Emergency Management Intranet GIS Application.

It works like this: when there's an earthquake of 4.0 or greater anywhere in the western United States, Caltech transmits data from strong motion detectors installed at over thirty SCE facilities statewide. Rather than being sent through phone lines, however, this emergency data is transmitted over dedicated communication lines. Because this method of data transmission relies on earth-orbiting satellites and not land-based wires, it's immune to earthquake damage and other natural disasters.

Data from the seismometers is fed into the EMIGA server, which runs it through an ArcView Spatial Analyst routine to generate map data showing ground acceleration contours (how much shaking, and where), and how these contours relate to SCE's service area, shown at right by a gray boundary. District management in Visalia, for instance, could see this map within moments of the earthquake and determine that their area was unaffected. They could use this information to decide whether to send crews south for emergency duty.

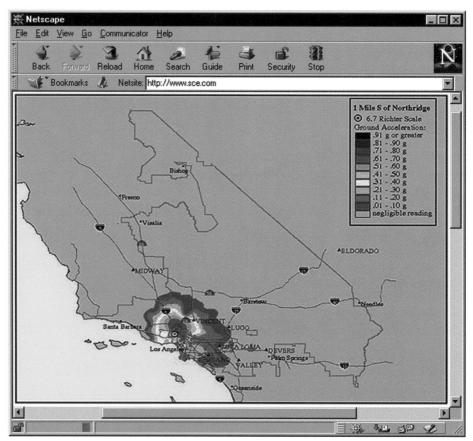

Within seconds of a 4.0 or greater earthquake, anyone logging on to SCE's secure intranet could examine the map above to see how severe the quake is and how it affects their area. In this map depicting data from the Northridge quake of 1994, the red areas reflect extreme shaking (and probably severe damage); orange means mild shaking and less damage; green indicates perceptible shaking, but little or no expected damage.

During an actual emergency

Managers close to the epicenter can zoom in to a more detailed view of the affected area. (The images at the right were created from data collected during the 1994 Northridge, California, earthquake.)

As the view is zoomed in further, additional layers of data showing major transportation corridors and Southern California Edison substations (the blue triangles) become visible. Remember, this data is available almost immediately after the event, so emergency response managers know the damage their crews might encounter as they're dispatched to the affected areas.

Other emergency management teams will use this same data to inform the local media about the situation. It is hoped that such rapid information sharing will help save lives and make damage repair easier and faster.

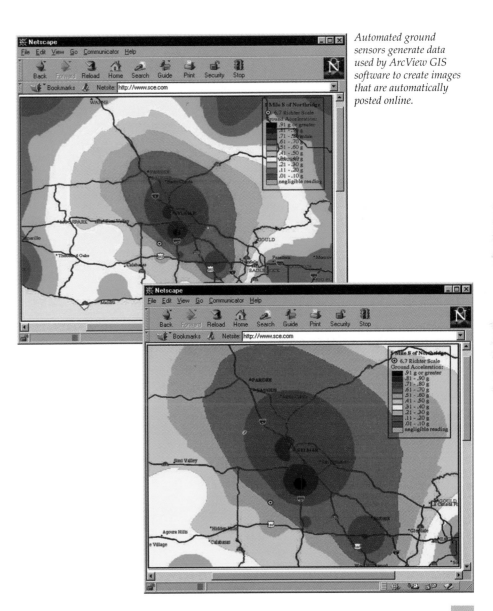

Automated ground sensors generate data used by ArcView GIS software to create images that are automatically posted online.

Data

Infrastructure data created and maintained by Southern California Edison.

Streets from Thomas Bros. Maps®.

Software

ArcView GIS

ArcView Spatial Analyst

ArcView Internet Map Server

Acknowledgments

Thanks to James Rodriguez and David Schirmer of Southern California Edison.

Chapter 4

A GIS on every desktop

Until recently, spatial literacy—the understanding of how geographic analysis can be used to solve a wide variety of problems—was limited to GIS experts running high-end systems like ARC/INFO software. In the past few years, however, much has changed. GIS data is now widely available and finding applications in virtually all aspects of society. More people now regularly access and use geographic information than ever before. GIS is well on its way to becoming as ubiquitous and widely understood as word processors and spreadsheets.

In this chapter, you'll learn how an Internet consulting firm installed ESRI's ArcExplorer™ GIS data viewer on every PC desktop in the company as a way of communicating the benefits of GIS throughout the organization.

Net gains

Tantalus Communications, Inc. (Vancouver, British Columbia), is a consulting firm that develops user-friendly information systems for its clients. Since its founding in 1994, the company has seen its projects gradually shift from desktop applications deployed on local area networks to enterprisewide projects running on Internet-based technology standards.

When one of its clients, the British Columbia Yellow Pages, awarded an important contract to Tantalus to help launch a map-based Web server, Tantalus management quickly realized that in order to get the work done, virtually their entire staff would have to be trained.

Tantalus Communications, Inc., operates its technology-based consulting business in scenic Vancouver, British Columbia.

The BC Yellow Pages project

The BC Telecom contract awarded to Tantalus involved creating and maintaining a map-based Web site, dubbed *bcyellowpages.com.*

Like many companies in the global telecommunications industry, BC Telecom has begun using the Internet as a way to improve service to existing clients and to create new business opportunities by, for example, transferring its existing yellow pages to the World Wide Web.

Tantalus' challenge was to create a database that would generate the dynamic maps to be served over the Internet. This meant using a variety of ESRI software, including ARC/INFO and Spatial Database Engine (SDE) software. Tantalus was also assigned the monumental task of geocoding (or correlating to a map location) the 150,000 business records provided by BC Telecom.

As the work got underway, the GIS department and the rest of the company realized that since almost everyone in the company would be handling GIS data files, they needed some way to communicate with one another about the work.

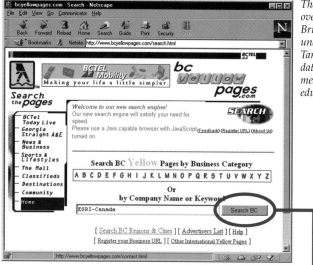

The BC Yellow Pages Web site lists over 150,000 business locations in British Columbia, Canada. Working under tight deadlines, the entire Tantalus workforce helped create the database that underlies this site. This meant that the entire staff had to be educated in the basics of spatial data.

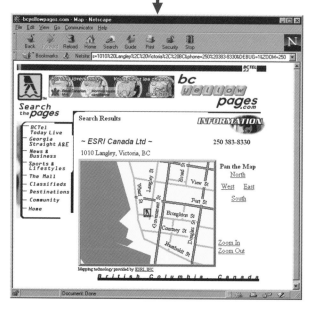

Increasing GIS literacy

The GIS department at Tantalus started out informally, showing the other employees what they were working on and explaining the problems they were facing. This method was partly successful, but some employees still considered GIS complicated and intimidating. What was missing was actual experience with the new technology. The GIS staff wanted to give everyone a copy of ArcView GIS software and provide the needed training, but that would have been expensive and time-consuming.

The solution arrived with the release of ESRI's free, downloadable ArcExplorer GIS data viewer. This viewing software offered the ability to browse and query GIS data through an easy-to-learn user interface. After downloading the program from ESRI's Web site (www.esri.com/arcexplorer), the GIS staff realized that this was exactly what they had been looking for. They quickly set up a companywide intranet system for sharing data and made the ArcExplorer viewer available to all employees.

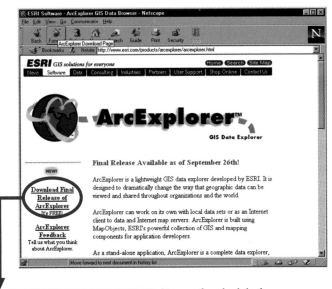

You can download the free ArcExplorer GIS data viewer at www.esri.com/arcexplorer.

ArcExplorer in action

The ArcExplorer data viewer was just the thing for introducing neophytes to GIS. It was easy to use, and its small footprint (the disk space it took up) meant it would run on any machine in the office.

After a little training, employees were soon exploring the GIS data files placed on the internal network.

The new users found it easy to pan and zoom around the data, turn various layers on and off, and point at features to bring up tables of additional information.

Tantalus' employees began to ask the GIS department questions about the data viewer and geographic information in general.

A few days into the process, the company's president called the GIS manager into his office. He had the ArcExplorer data viewer running on his own PC with almost every possible theme active. The communication problem had vanished; with GIS, the entire staff could now discuss the project in a common framework.

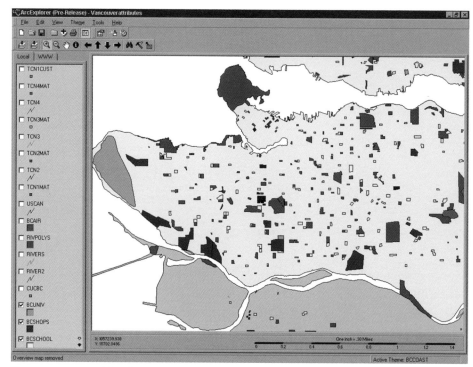

To expose everyone within their organization to GIS, Tantalus management placed a wealth of local spatial data on the company's intranet and installed ArcExplorer software on every desktop.

Incorporating maps in other documents

Various departments at Tantalus now use the ArcExplorer data viewer for all sorts of things. Sales staff use it to demonstrate GIS applications to potential clients; management uses it to produce maps for project proposals; the quality control group uses it to monitor the accuracy of edits made to the BC Yellow Pages databases.

In addition, the marketing department incorporated maps created with the software into a plan that touted the company's GIS capabilities to customers.

In the months that followed, Tantalus used the data viewer to teach courses at Simon Fraser University and prepare graphics for a variety of other projects. Even the summer interns were seen looking up directions to local pubs with the program.

The ArcExplorer data viewer has allowed everyone at Tantalus Communications to realize that GIS is simply a logical extension of a normal database.

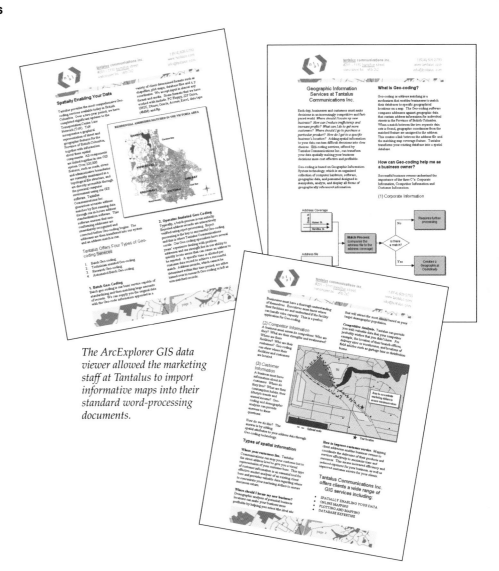

The ArcExplorer GIS data viewer allowed the marketing staff at Tantalus to import informative maps into their standard word-processing documents.

Data

Street data from the British Columbia Ministry of Highways.

Other data from *Data & Maps* CD–ROM (included with ArcView GIS software), ESRI.

Software

ArcExplorer

ArcView GIS

Spatial Database Engine and ARC/INFO (for the bcyellowpages.com project)

Acknowledgments

Thanks to Mark Allen and Tom Munro of Tantalus Communications, Inc.

The Yellow Pages is a registered trademark of Tele-Direct Publications, Inc. BC Telecom is a licensed user.

Chapter 5

Building an Internet-based spatial data library

A spatial data library is a collection of databases containing geographically referenced information. Once confined to internal networks at large government institutions, spatial data libraries are now finding a place on the Internet, and getting much more use than ever before. By publishing their spatial data libraries on the Internet, an increasing number of government agencies are more closely in touch with the people than ever before.

In this chapter you'll see how the federal agency that coordinates the protection of America's coastal resources created a Web-based tool for accessing its huge spatial data library.

Managing coastal resources

A part of the National Oceanic and Atmospheric Administration (NOAA), the National Ocean Service (NOS) is the primary agency within the federal government responsible for the health, safety, and wise use of our nation's coasts.

NOS gathers data with cutting-edge technology and uses it to produce the marine and aeronautical charts needed for safe navigation. NOS also provides data to private companies and government agencies. NOS recently completed the first phase of a plan to publish its core databases of coastal information online.

The work of the National Ocean Service encompasses a broad range of activities including shipping, defense, weather forecasting, tourism, and education.

The MapFinder project

The MapFinder project started out simply as a way to get maps, aerial photographs, and other spatial data to traditional users of NOS data. But because the Web is accessible to anyone connected to the Internet, the project has turned out to be an outreach effort, one more example of technology making government more accessible to citizens. The system's target users are resource managers (municipal planners, protected-area managers, and so on), but the information and product offerings also benefit a much wider audience. For example, NOS data now finds its way into college term papers, citizens' activist projects, and even sixth-grade science fairs.

MapFinder offers immediate access to a variety of NOS products on a single World Wide Web site. This map-based interface allows users to select a local or regional area of interest, find out what information and products are available for that area, and download specific products. Additionally, the service provides background information known as metadata for each class of data so that users can better understand the source, methods, quality, and limitations of specific products.

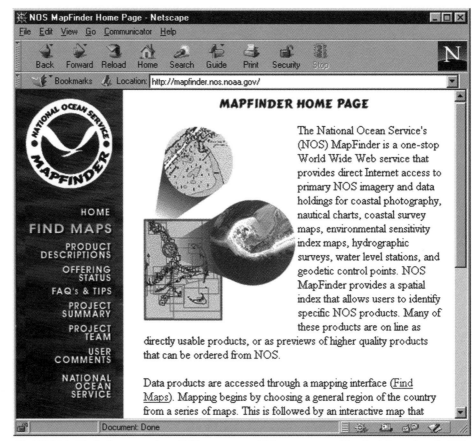

The NOS MapFinder home page is available to anyone with Internet access. The site is located on the Web at mapfinder.nos.noaa.gov.

Building a local database

A local government analyst in Key Bis-cayne, Florida, is creating a GIS database as part of a larger effort to modernize his agency's information systems. He has already acquired most of the land-based records he needs from other regional agencies, but he still needs some detailed coastal information since Key Biscayne is really an island just off Miami.

Before MapFinder, he would have placed an order by phone with the NOS data staff. After a week or two, the data on a CD–ROM would show up in the mail and he'd be ready to go.

Now he just points his browser to the URL mapfinder.nos.noaa.gov and downloads what he needs that very same day. Time, effort, and money are saved on both sides of the transaction.

Now let's examine the process he went through to select and retrieve the data.

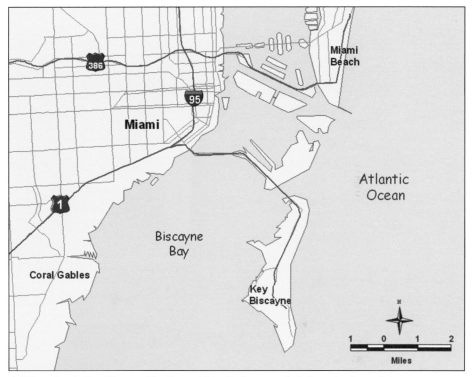

A GIS analyst in Key Biscayne, Florida, used MapFinder to get the information he needed.

Finding a region

From the MapFinder home page, a single mouse click takes the analyst to the Region Selection module. Clicking on the southern tip of Florida brings up a detailed map of the southern Florida coastline. From here he selects Zoom In and clicks a few more steps to the place on the map where Key Biscayne is located.

Once the map is zoomed in sufficiently to cover only his area of interest, the analyst looks at the list of data products currently available through the system and places checkmarks by the ones he wants.

After specifying that he wants data only from a certain timeframe, and then restricting the selection to immediately available data sets, he chooses Find Data in the Navigation tools.

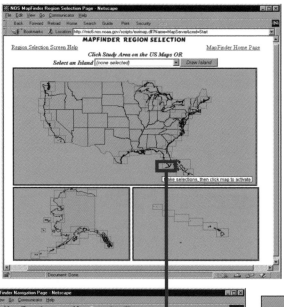

The red arrows show where to point on the map to zoom in; the blue arrow shows where to specify the desired data and access metadata for each theme; the green arrow shows where to choose the time window; and the yellow arrow points to a check box that restricts the search to downloadable data only.

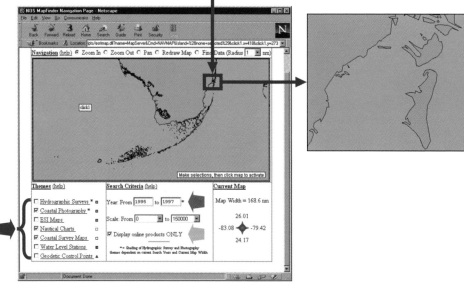

Data and product offerings

The analyst next examines the available data from the following choices:

Hydrographic surveys measure and define the bottoms and adjacent land areas of water bodies, especially as they pertain to navigation.

Georeferenced, high-resolution *coastal photography* is used to show the shoreline and man-made features.

Environmental Sensitivity Index (ESI) maps identify areas most vulnerable to ecological damage in the event of oil spills or other disasters.

Coastal survey maps depict the shoreline and shoreline features such as rocks and tidal flats.

Nautical charts are fundamental navigational tools. They also serve as base maps for planning shoreline development.

Water level stations provide the basic tidal data used to determine U.S. coastal marine boundaries and are also used to create and update nautical charts.

Geodetic control points define latitude, longitude, elevation, scale, gravity, and orientation, and how these values change with time.

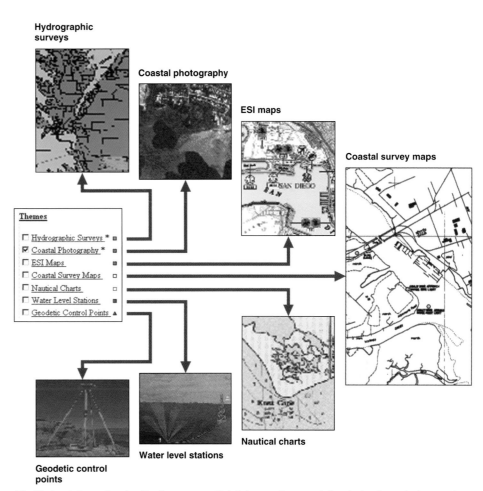

The National Ocean Service distributes many digital data products needed to depict the nation's coastal environments.

The results module

After he's identified and selected several themes of interest, the analyst is presented with a list showing all available data sets.

A series of icons tells him that digital GIF image files are available for three of the four available data sets returned from his query. He clicks on the green GIF icon to bring up the high-resolution images for each. Using his Web browser's *Save image as…* command, he saves them all to the hard drive on his computer. One file (the Key Biscayne S. coastal photograph) is not yet online. In this case, clicking on the order icon provides a sample image and instructions for ordering the product.

Before logging off from MapFinder, the analyst accesses the metadata system and downloads the data about his data. In addition to the metadata, an extensive help system is also just a click away.

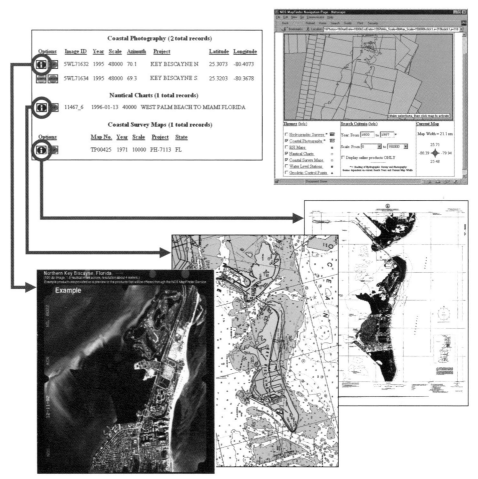

The list from the initial query tells the analyst how to view and retrieve the data.

The help system and support material

The help system is an integral part of MapFinder. It's really an online training module for using MapFinder.

Linked to the help system is the built-in metadata component of MapFinder. Extensive product descriptions are accessible from either the home page or the theme selection section of the system. For each theme, a description, an annotated product example, and metadata are available. Metadata, presented in the form of a simple text file, is essentially the pedigree of the data. Without this information, the spatial data is of little use. In addition to such critical details as when and how the data was obtained, metadata also gives useful information like the projection of the data and the agency responsible for its upkeep.

Thus, the analyst in Florida has successfully acquired the data he needs in the space of an hour, as opposed to the days or weeks it might have taken him before. He's able to get on with his real work, as are the NOS administrators, who are no longer spending as much time fulfilling individual data orders.

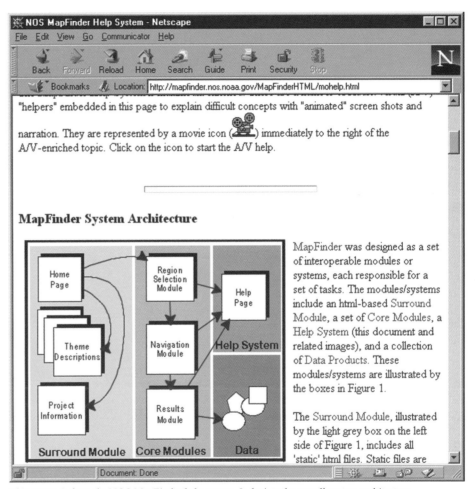

This screen is from the NOS MapFinder help system. It depicts the overall system architecture.

Data

All of the data included on the NOS MapFinder Web site was collected and maintained by one of the following NOS operational units:

Office of Ocean Resources Conservation and Assessment

Office of Ocean and Coastal Resource Management

National Geodetic Survey

Office of Aeronautical Charting

Office of Coast Survey

Coastal Services Center

Software

MapObjects

ARC/INFO

Spatial Database Engine

Acknowledgments

Thanks to Russ Perry of the National Ocean Service.

Chapter 6

•••••• N a t i o n a l   r e a l   e s t a t e   f i n d e r

Looking for a new home used to be a time-consuming process. Using local newspapers and real estate agents, you'd identify the houses you could afford. You'd then start driving through neighborhoods trying to figure out how far you were from schools, shopping, and work, and how long it would take to get to the nearest freeway. All the while, lamenting that the houses for sale never looked as nice as the ones already sold. No more. That is, though the sold houses will always look better, the Internet can eliminate much of the drudgery of finding a new home.

In this chapter, you'll see how the Internet's busiest and largest interactive real estate Web site, built by a national organization of real estate professionals, has transformed the age-old ritual of house hunting into an almost pleasurable experience.

Location, location, location

RealSelect, Inc. (Westlake Village, California), has developed a highly sophisticated real estate Web site for its sponsoring organization, the National Association of Realtors (NAR).

Founded in 1908, NAR is now the world's largest trade organization, with 720,000 members. Composed of residential and commercial Realtors, property managers, and appraisers, NAR membership is filled with people keen to use new technology.

NAR continues its tradition of distributing high-tech tools to its members in the form of its Web site, Realtor.com.

Finding the perfect home is among life's most exciting, yet agonizing, experiences. Map-based Web sites are finally making that process a little more friendly.

Before Realtor.com

Before Realtor.com, the search for a suitable home in a new city could very well begin with a flurry of phone calls, followed by a tedious wait for listings to arrive in the mail. The result would be a rushed trip to a strange town and the pressure of making a big decision quickly.

Alternatively, you might pack a suitcase, find a cheap apartment in your new town, and spend your lunch hours looking at houses and your evenings at home on the phone and leafing through countless real estate brochures.

Realtor.com is located on the World Wide Web at www.realtor.com.

Beginning the search

No more. With Realtor.com, from the comfort of your home, you can type in www.realtor.com (or just realtor.com) and zoom to an area (in this case Southern California) by clicking on a map of the United States. From here you have access to the entire NAR database of home listings. In minutes, you will have accomplished more than you could have done in weeks.

Maps offer a natural and intuitive means of accessing geographic information.

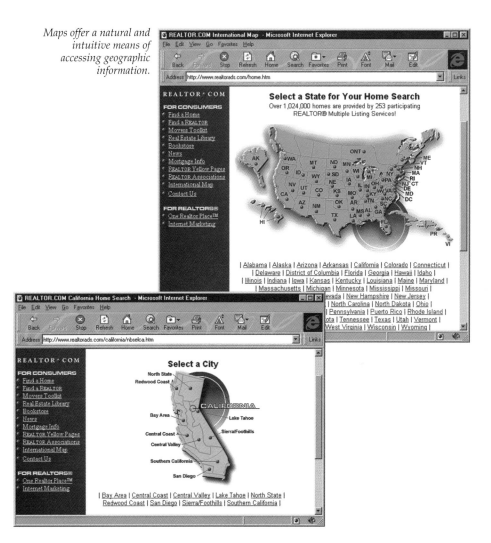

Making a specific query

Suppose you and your family are going to move close to the Pacific Ocean. Zoom in to the southern coastal region of California, and a list of cities in Orange County pops up. Narrow your search to a list of suitable houses by completing a detailed checklist. You can set the price range, choose the number of bedrooms and bathrooms, and select such options as hardwood floors, a garage, and even an ocean view.

A few clicks on these well-designed pages bring the user to a query screen where you can specify all the amenities you want in a house.

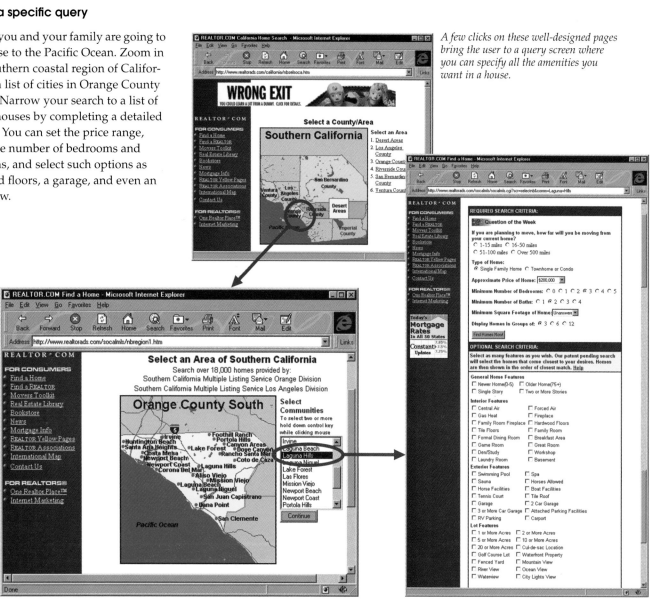

Results

Your initial search finds only four houses, but number three looks appealing. You click to get more information and to "Map It." The house is smaller than you wanted, but does have a view of the ocean. After spending a few more minutes trying different combinations of criteria, and even different towns in the Irvine area, you are ready to head to California and look at some houses.

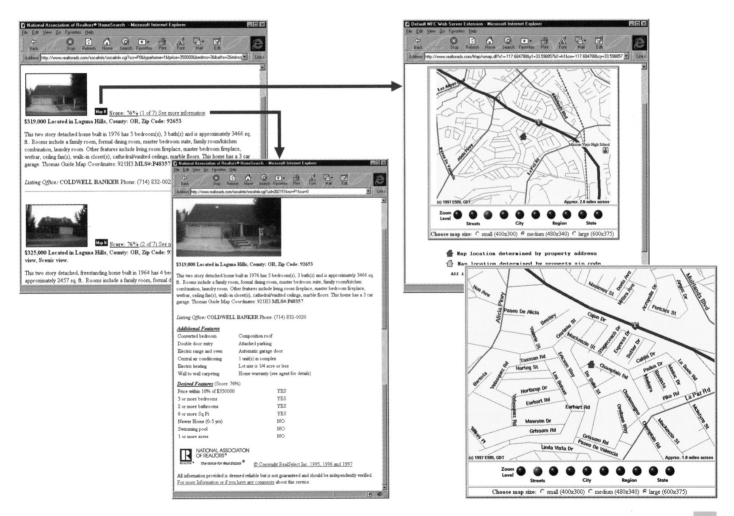

Banner ads and links

Now you're here. Now what?

You just click on the Realtor Yellow Pages to bring up a query window. By typing in the city name "Laguna Hills," you get a list of brokers in that part of Orange County. The same Web page also features a banner ad for a specific Century 21® agent in Laguna Hills. You click on the ad and get the e-mail address for the agent.

Realtor.com accepts banner ads and has programmed the site so that advertising is appropriately matched to user input. In addition to providing some of the revenue needed to run the site, these ad links also provide you with information tailored to your specific needs.

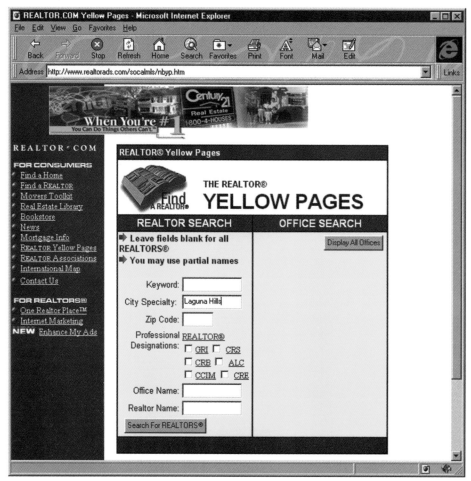

The Realtor Yellow Pages put you in touch with real agents.

Data

Dynamap/2000® from GDT

Software

MapObjects Internet Map Server

Spatial Database Engine

Acknowledgments

Thanks to Richard Janssen of
RealSelect, Inc.

Chapter 7

Bioregional geographic information server

When it comes to ecology, there's really no such thing as a local problem. Watersheds in one area are affected by logging hundreds of miles away, housing development in one town reduces the habitat for a species that ranges over an area covering several states. In the past, organizations trying to solve local environmental problems were hard-pressed to get scientific information about the big picture.

In this chapter, you'll see how a nonprofit conservation group encourages regions to share information with each other, and how it has used the Internet to make that information widely available.

Sharing data for the common good

Interrain Pacific (Portland, Oregon) is an independent, nonprofit organization dedicated to promoting environmentally conscious development in the coastal rain forest that extends from southern Alaska to northern California. Through intelligent application of computer technology and partnerships with other organizations and vendors, Interrain is making a name for itself in high-tech ecological management.

By making data on social and ecological changes available to all the local organizations and communities in this region, Interrain Pacific hopes to provide the means for solving problems that ignore local boundaries.

Courtesy of
WorldSat
International, Inc.

Interrain Pacific helps local agencies get environmental data for any part of North America's west coast.

The INFORAIN Web site

Realizing that Internet and computer technology could significantly advance their efforts, Interrain Pacific set up a special Web site known as INFORAIN. This site (located at www.inforain.org) is the core of the organization's information system for the temperate rain forest of North America's west coast.

Initially, Interrain wanted to create a network of accessible and useful information at multiple map scales; information about the environment, changes in the landscape over time, and man-made features (infrastructure). This would help organizations, individuals, and businesses get information relevant to their local concerns. At the site, people can discuss issues via online forums and conferences; look at social, economic, and environmental trends; read the latest news; download data or the results of data analysis; and link to other Web sites.

The most active area of the Web site has been the Mapping section, where people can use interactive maps or download data and satellite images.

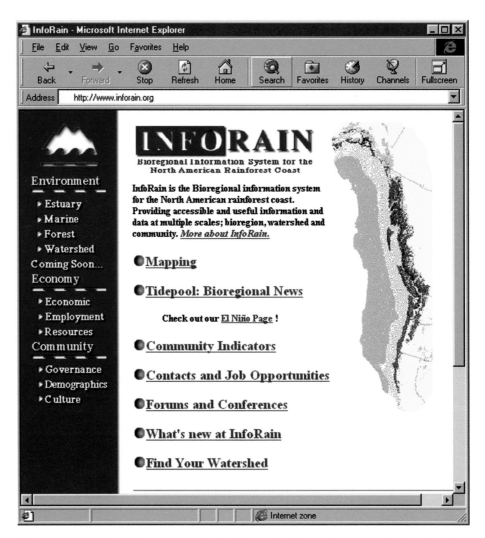

The INFORAIN Web site is the starting point for Interrain Pacific's ambitious project designed to get environmental data into the hands of community and business leaders.

What data is available

Four types of information are available: GIS data sets, satellite imagery, animated fly-bys, and online mapping.

Suppose you're a scientist interested in studying the Oregon coastline. You point your browser to www.inforain.org and click on mapping, then Oregon to bring up a list of links to Oregon geographic information.

Under each of the main headings, the Interrain system lists the data available for Oregon. The items in these lists are, in fact, links that will take you to a place where you can learn more about the data and download it if it meets your needs.

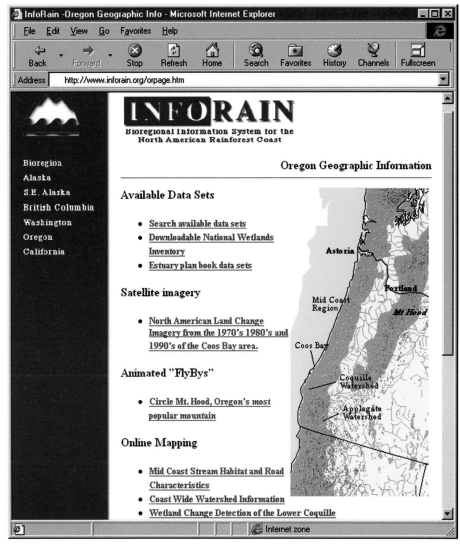

The INFORAIN section on Oregon presents a list of data for that region. This includes traditional GIS vector files, as well as satellite images, animated "fly-bys," and interactive mapping applications.

GIS data layers

Interrain Pacific has an extensive database of GIS data layers describing just about every natural and man-made feature of the local geography. It includes everything from logging roads and vegetation cover to snapshots of wetlands as they existed at different times.

By clicking on the name "nwi.mc" in the list of available GIS data sets, you begin the process of downloading the file from the Interrain server to your local machine. This particular file happens to be a GIS database of wetlands classifications collected by the National Wetlands Inventory.

Once you've downloaded the file, you can use a program like ArcExplorer or ArcView GIS software (seen here) to create a map of wetlands. Using the metadata, you decode the attribute data associated with each record in the shapefile to create a thematic map. The map at the right, for example, assigns different colors to the wetlands according to primary classifications such as palustrine, lacustrine, and so forth. The database also includes more detailed classifications that can be used to create dozens of different thematic maps of the same geographic area.

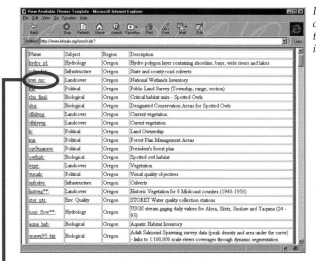

Interrain offers a growing list of GIS data sets, including the downloadable wetlands inventories mapped here.

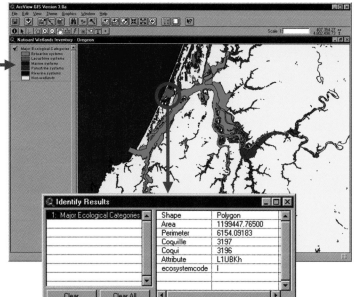

Satellite imagery

Satellite imagery is another important source of data for the scientific community, and one that has historically been more difficult to obtain than other types of data. Thanks to relaxed laws regarding the distribution of satellite images, the Interrain site has a large sample of this remote sensing data available on its Web site.

Remote sensing is the technical name for acquiring data from a distance, in this case a distance of some 10 to 20 miles in space. Remotely sensed data can be "image processed," or analyzed using computer models, to create digital GIS data, like this map of old growth forest for a strip of central Oregon coastline (below right).

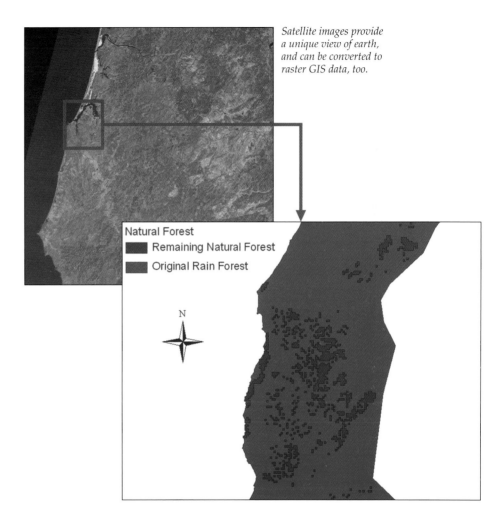

Satellite images provide a unique view of earth, and can be converted to raster GIS data, too.

Natural Forest
■ Remaining Natural Forest
■ Original Rain Forest

N

Online mapping

By now you've downloaded several megabytes of data. You'd like to look at some of the other data sets, but don't have time to download them. So instead, you click to the part of the system called "Online Mapping."

This part of the system uses ESRI's ArcView Internet Map Server (IMS) software, and a Java program that comes with it, to set up a user-controlled map window.

Without having to download any data, you navigate to your areas of interest and select some layers to display. After a bit of tweaking, you manage to create a number of maps depicting land use, infrastructure, and wetlands change over time. You can save these maps as image files to print out or include in a report.

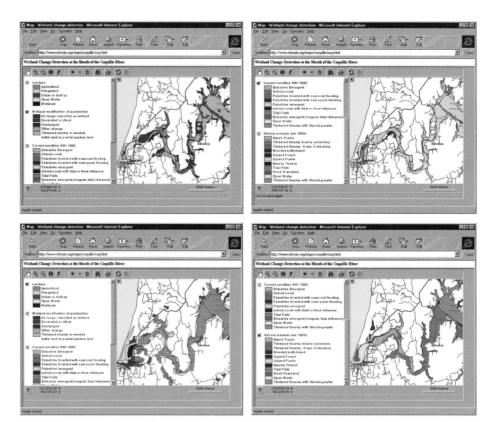

The online mapping feature of the INFORAIN system uses an interactive Java applet that allows the user to create maps over the Internet. The maps are then easily saved as image files.

Animated fly-bys

Finally, you check out a brief animated fly-by movie of Mt. Hood, Oregon, created in VRML (Virtual Reality Modeling Language).

VRML fly-bys are movies created one frame at a time by draping satellite photos or other image data over digital elevation models of terrain. Played one after another like an old flip-card movie, these files simulate the effect of flying over the landscape.

After saving the movie on your local drive, you log off the INFORAIN system. In the course of about an hour, you have downloaded several GIS data files, created online maps, and taken a virtual tour of Mt. Hood.

Before INFORAIN, arranging to get even some of this data would have taken at least a day of phone calls and e-mail, and you would have then had to wait another several days to actually receive the data from the different agencies that produced it.

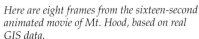

Here are eight frames from the sixteen-second animated movie of Mt. Hood, based on real GIS data.

Data

The INFORAIN Web site contains data from dozens of federal, state, and regional agencies. The data used to illustrate this chapter includes the following:

National Wetlands Inventory was prepared by the U.S. Department of Interior, Fish and Wildlife Service, Washington, D.C.

Aquatic habitat data was compiled from the Bureau of Land Management, Oregon Department of Forestry, Oregon Department of Fish and Wildlife, Oregon Forest Industries Council, and the Siuslaw National Forest.

Historic wetlands data was mapped by Patricia Benner, interpreting land survey notes circa 1857–1872.

North American Landscape Characterization satellite images were provided by the U.S. Landsat program.

Three-dimensional image of western North America on page 55 is used with permission of WorldSat International, Inc., Mississauga, Ontario, Canada.

Software

ArcView Internet Map Server

MapCafé™ Java applet

MapObjects Internet Map Server

ARC/INFO version 7.1

Acknowledgments

Thanks to Mike Mertens of Interrain Pacific.

Chapter 8

Airport noise and the community

As residential neighborhoods are built closer and closer to metropolitan airports, jet noise is becoming a significant problem. Studying the noise impact of flight operations on surrounding communities is a classic application of GIS thinking: it has a spatial component (in this case, a three-dimensional space), it has a temporal component, and it's best communicated with a map.

In this chapter you'll see how a major international airport has set up an interactive, map-based Web site to disseminate noise level data gathered from remote listening stations and flight track information from FAA radar. More importantly, you'll see how the public is benefiting from the new technology.

Breaking the sound barrier

Minneapolis–St. Paul International Airport in Minnesota is owned and operated by the Metropolitan Airports Commission (MAC). In 1996, thirty-two million passengers were accommodated at the airport, where nearly 1,350 planes land or depart daily.

Because this airport is located near the center of the Minneapolis–St. Paul urban area, the commission is especially sensitive to the impact of its operations on the surrounding community.

So, as part of its program to provide noise and flight track information to the community, MAC put most of its aircraft noise data on the World Wide Web with the help of some innovative GIS applications.

Noise generated by a jet airplane on takeoff can easily exceed 100 decibels as measured from the ground. As urban areas continue to grow closer to major U.S. airports, the impact of this noise on the population is being taken more seriously.

Looking for noise

Suppose you have an opportunity to buy some vacant industrial land in downtown Minneapolis. The city offers generous redevelopment incentives that make the construction of an apartment complex on the site seem like a good investment.

The only drawback you can identify is that the location is just 2 miles from the Minneapolis–St. Paul International Airport. You're concerned about the noise levels in the area. How do you find out what they are?

After walking the site and listening as several jets fly overhead, you conclude that the noise levels are loud, but not too loud. You wish, however, that you had more evidence than just your own impression.

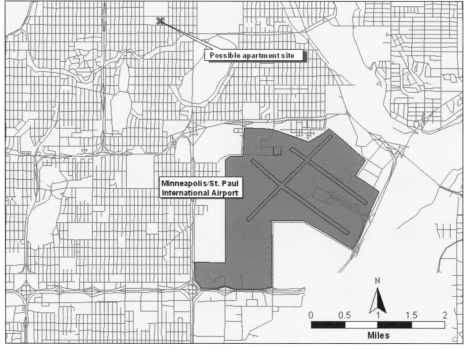

Scenario: a tract of land in south Minneapolis has been cleared by the city council for redevelopment. Will the noise from aircraft takeoffs and landings annoy residents if an apartment is built there?

Complaint tracking

The commission's GIS site has links to several aircraft noise and approach databases. One of these plots each noise complaint as a point on a map, thereby giving a visual representation of the parts of the city where residents have registered the most complaints.

The purple dots in the graphic show that most complaints come from the area directly under the flight path. Unfortunately, this also happens to be where the land you're thinking of buying is located.

Upon closer inspection, however, you realize that the parcel you're interested in lies in a gap between two of the largest clusters of complaints. Maybe the noise is not as bad in this "sweet spot" as in adjacent areas. Still, it would be helpful to have more data.

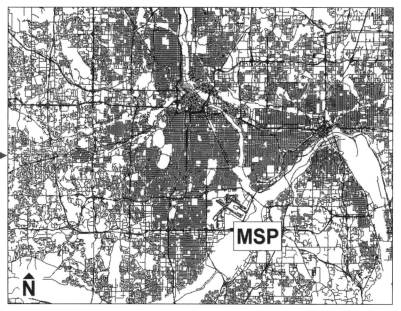

Updated monthly, this map shows the origin of noise complaints logged by the airport commission.

Measuring aircraft noise

The Federal Aviation Authority (FAA) has mandated that metropolitan airports in the United States continually measure aircraft noise from the ground.

In compliance, MAC has deployed a series of unmanned monitoring stations to record the times and decibel levels of aircraft takeoffs and departures. Located throughout the surrounding communities, and linked to the airport Web page through an automated GIS application, the stations now provide daily noise levels for all parts of the city.

Clicking on the purple symbols representing Remote Monitoring Stations 4 and 6 (the ones closest to the land parcel in question) presents you with maps of the listening devices and tables showing peak and average noise levels in decibels.

By comparing the levels from the monitors nearest your site with others around town, you determine that while the site does sustain above-average noise levels, it's not nearly as loud as other residential neighborhoods closer to the airport. That's good news. Taking your investigation a step farther, you might like to find out just how close the planes fly overhead.

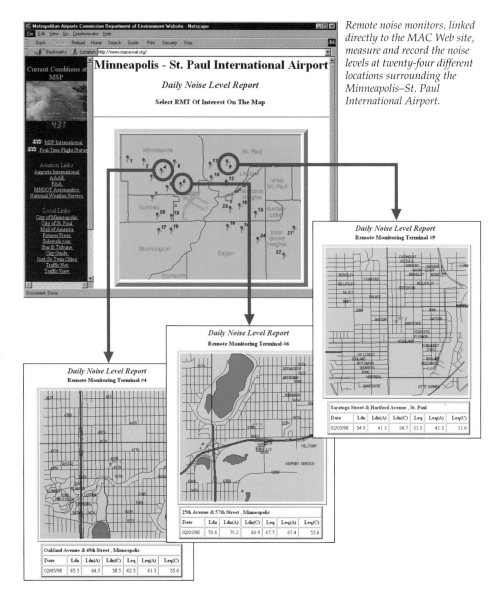

Remote noise monitors, linked directly to the MAC Web site, measure and record the noise levels at twenty-four different locations surrounding the Minneapolis–St. Paul International Airport.

Point of Closest Approach

Another database that forms part of the system is the commission's Point of Closest Approach (PCA) database. The data is time-stamped, so you can get information about all flights for any given day. (PCA measures straight-line distance, not simply vertical distance.)

This database tracks the complete flight path of every takeoff and landing at the airport. Supplied with a street address, the system returns a table listing the vectors, or paths, of each flight and a map with a red bubble at the point of closest approach for each flight.

You pick the date for a recent weekday morning and run a check for your site and a few others for comparison. It turns out that the points of closest approach at your site are well over 3,000 feet. In contrast, a location within 1 mile of the airport (seen at right) experiences flyovers as close at 1,600 feet.

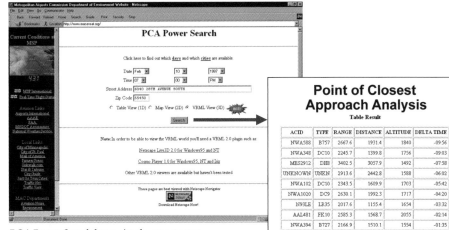

PCA Power Search has a simple, easy-to-use interface. By typing a street address and picking a time window, you can see the point of closest approach to that address for all flights.

Point of Closest Approach Analysis

Table Result

ACID	TYPE	RANGE	DISTANCE	ALTITUDE	DELTA TIME
NWA588	B757	2667.6	1931.4	1840	-09:56
NWA348	DC10	2245.7	1399.8	1756	-09:03
MES2912	DH8	3402.5	3057.9	1492	-07:58
UNKNOWN	UNKN	2913.6	2442.8	1588	-06:02
NWA102	DC10	2343.5	1609.9	1703	-05:42
NWA1020	DC9	2630.1	1992.3	1717	-04:20
N93LE	LR35	2017.6	1155.4	1654	-03:32
AAL481	FK10	2585.3	1568.7	2055	-02:14
NWA394	B727	2166.9	1510.1	1554	-01:35
FLG859	BA31	2949.8	2532.8	1512	-00:04
FLG857	BA31	2523.5	1912.7	1646	+00:29
NWA1767	EA32	2509.1	1952.4	1576	+01:08
FLG845	SF34	2474.1	1670.4	1825	+01:42
NWA1080	DC9	2130.2	1611.6	1393	+02:09

✈ 6040 28TH AVE S 55450

◆ rmts ▪ track points

Visualizing the flight paths

Because airspace is three-dimensional, the same data can be viewed more realistically in VRML, or Virtual Reality Modeling Language, which creates a simulated 3-D environment. With a VRML viewer (like Cosmo™ Player, seen here), you can change your perspective by rotating the entire data set to any horizontal and vertical angle. The two-dimensional graphics on this page do not really do the effect justice, as you can do by visiting the site for yourself.

The MAC Web site is an excellent example of an agency putting its best foot forward. Whereas not long ago, this type of data was locked up in mainframe computers away from the public eye, today it's in a public place where people can readily find and use it. The feedback that the commission has gotten from the community has bolstered its resolve to continue to expand and improve the Web site.

And, thanks to MAC, you can go ahead and complete that real estate deal.

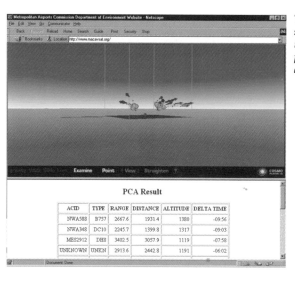

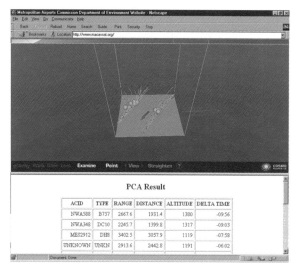

The 3-D graphics at the left show some frames of the VRML views of the data. The yellow spheres represent points of closest approach to a specific address on the ground.

The airport's Web site

The Minneapolis–St. Paul International Airport Web site offers much more than information about noise. The site offers a wealth of information that makes life easier for the millions of people who fly in and out of the airport monthly.

For example, from the main airport Web page, users planning trips to Minneapolis can link to a current weather report and satellite map. They can also pull up a map of the entire airport to help them find where to catch a cab or meet Aunt Mabel.

A service dubbed FlightTracker promises to end the age-old headache of calling the airline to check the status of a particular flight. Give FlightTracker the exact flight number, and the system tells you when the plane took off and when it's supposed to land. It even displays a map with a superimposed plane signifying the aircraft's actual progress.

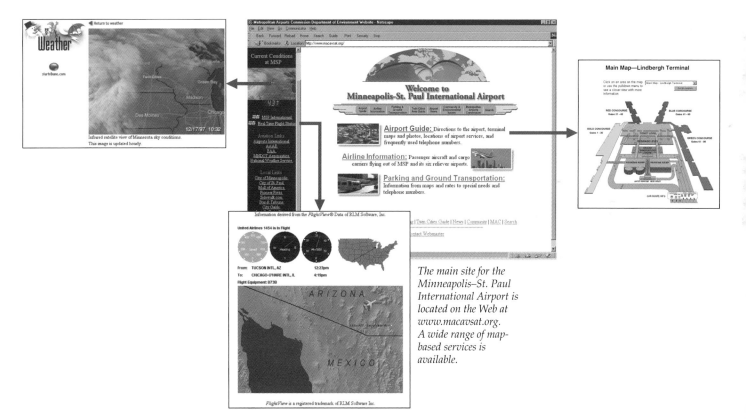

The main site for the Minneapolis–St. Paul International Airport is located on the Web at www.macavsat.org. A wide range of map-based services is available.

Technical configuration of the system

The commission's Internet map server is a Sun Microsystems™ Ultra™ 1 workstation with 512 megabytes of memory.

Each day, the remote sensing stations around the airport generate approximately 32MB of spatial data, which is automatically loaded into an ESRI Spatial Database Engine (SDE) and Oracle® database configuration. With a gigabyte of storage, the server holds about thirty days' worth of data. Each day when the new data is loaded, the oldest data is removed from the server and archived to make room for the new.

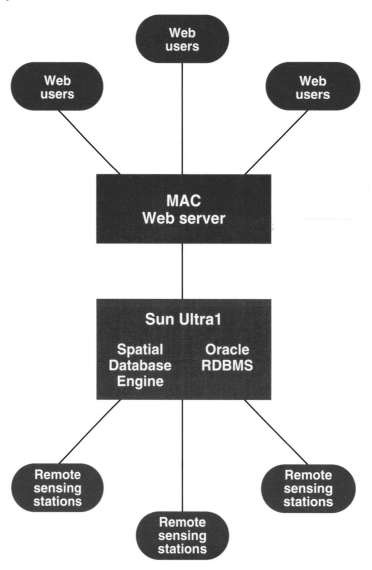

Acknowledgments

Thanks to the Aviation Noise and Satellite Programs Office, and, especially, to Dan Pfeffer of the Metropolitan Airports Commission.

Minneapolis-St. Paul International Airport
Metropolitan Airports Commission

Chapter 9

•••••• **S e r v i c e   t e c h n i c i a n   r o u t i n g**

For organizations that employ legions of mobile service technicians, using computers to automate the complex sequencing of their routes can boost productivity tremendously. For large operations, the difference between a poorly planned route and a well-planned one can be measured in millions of dollars (not to mention greatly improved customer satisfaction). GIS analysis of transportation networks coupled with intranet access to the information has allowed many service organizations to fully realize those benefits.

In this chapter, you'll see an application developed for a large gas utility to automate routes for its service technicians, and you'll see how putting the system on the company intranet will greatly improve its routing operations.

Glad to be of service℠

Southern California Gas Company (Los Angeles, California) is the largest distributor of natural gas in the United States, serving over seventeen million people through some 45,000 miles of distribution and transmission pipelines.

Unlike telephone or electric service, which can be switched on and off from a central location, the nature of gas service dictates that technicians must go where it's being delivered. Over 1,000 of the company's more than 7,000 employees work as customer service technicians.

For this reason, managers use the latest information technology (like GIS and the Internet) to do the best job possible in keeping the field work organized.

Southern California Gas Company uses advanced information technology including handheld computers and GIS to route field service technicians more efficiently.

Where it all starts

The standard way for customers to request service is to telephone SoCalGas. To better serve its busy (and increasingly Internet-connected) customers, the company recently added a new way to schedule a service visit: the World Wide Web. By logging onto the SoCalGas Web site at www.socalgas.com, customers can now submit their requests online, at any time of day or night.

SoCalGas receives thousands of requests for service each day: requests to have the gas turned on when someone moves into a new home or business or turned off when someone moves out, requests for gas appliance repairs and adjustments, and even requests to have pilots lit.

SoCalGas operates 52 service facilities in five regions. Each of these facilities employs anywhere from 20 to 50 service technicians, and each technician handles between 20 and 60 service calls per day. With this many people on the road, the company wants its routes to be as efficient as possible.

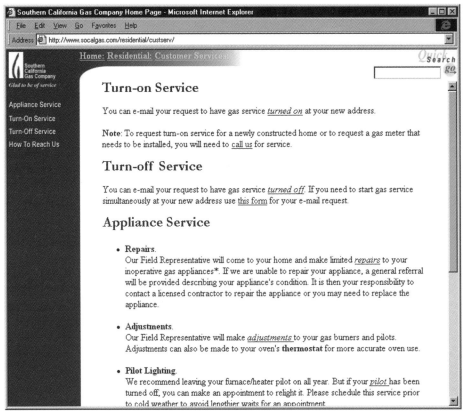

You can go to the SoCalGas Web site to ask that your gas be turned on or off.

The magic of automated routing

The service requests are stored as database records in a mainframe information system called PACER. SoCalGas employees known as routers group these service orders into routes and download them to the Geographic Routing and Integrated Dispatch (GRID) system. Each service order includes the type of job, the address of the home or business requiring service, and the estimated amount of time required to do the work.

A computer model of streets covering the company's entire service area is stored in the GRID system. Using ESRI's NetEngine™ technology, the GRID application considers all the stops on each technician's route and arranges them in the best visiting order. Sophisticated software algorithms take into account everything about the street network that will affect the route planning, like one-way streets and speed limits.

Once all the stops that have been assigned to a technician are sequenced, the service orders are downloaded to handheld computers for the next day, and also converted to shapefile paths. These are automatically loaded into an ArcView Internet Map Server application for serving over the company's internal network, or intranet.

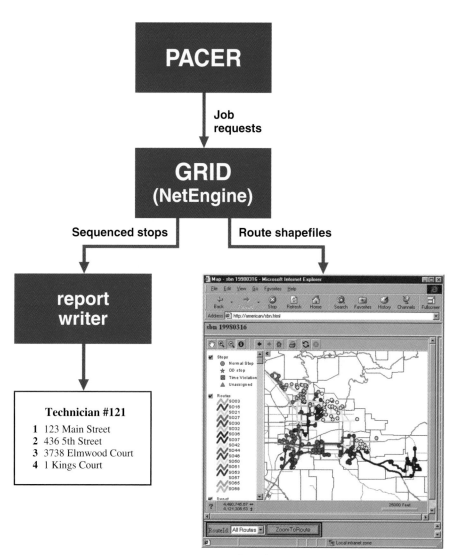

ArcView Internet Map Server

The map interface

The finished routes for each service technician can be displayed as different-colored paths on a street map.

Once the route maps have been put online via the intranet, the routers will be able to check the work in their Web browsers to make sure it makes logical sense. If anything seems amiss, the router can change it and reload the Web page to see the update. In fact, the ability to get to the route information using only a Web browser and no additional GIS software will make it much easier for all levels of SoCalGas administration to understand the routing function.

For each service facility, the default view is zoomed out to an extent wide enough to include all the routes. The tools across the top of the map allow users to zoom in on specific areas, pan the map, and query the data behind the routes.

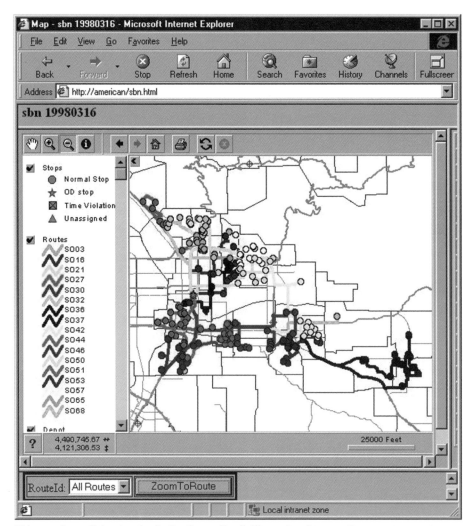

This map shows all the stops for the San Bernardino facility, assigned to more than seventeen routes.

Looking at a single route

Using the popup list at the bottom of the interface, a supervisor overseeing a team of technicians can easily select a single route (in this case, route 36). The map server then redraws the map with only that route displayed and changes the extent to cover just the geographic area of the single route.

The route is drawn in a color that contrasts with the streets, and the stops are shown as numbered dots that correspond to the locations where the technician will be working. Zooming in to one route turns on street labels.

Once the map in the Web browser window is zoomed in close enough to make individual stops discernible, the supervisor can select the Identify tool and get more information from the route database directly through the browser.

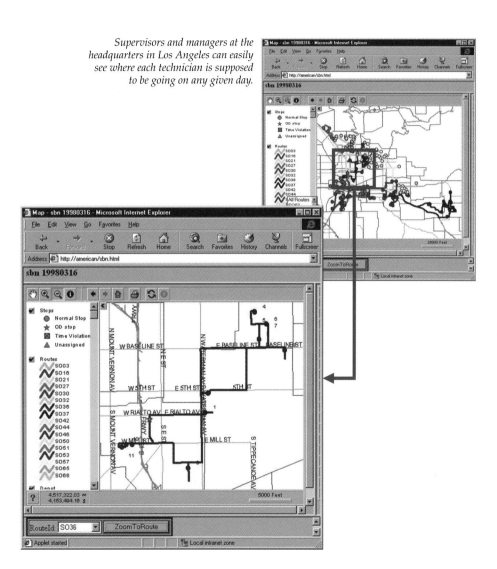

Supervisors and managers at the headquarters in Los Angeles can easily see where each technician is supposed to be going on any given day.

Identifying routes and stops

The Identify tool is one of the most useful features of the interface. Supervisors need only point and click on a route or a stop to bring up its associated information. This is significant because it means they can access all the information they need through the Web browser, instead of having to run separate routines on various software packages.

Presented in a table in the Web browser to the right of the map, this information includes a number of details about the routes and stops. For example, the route table seen in the lower graphic tells the supervisor, among other things, that the route is about 17 miles long, has eighteen stops, and should take the technician 393 minutes (about six and a half hours) to complete.

Clicking the Identify tool on a stop tells the supervisor its address, its distance from the previous stop, and the type of work to be performed there.

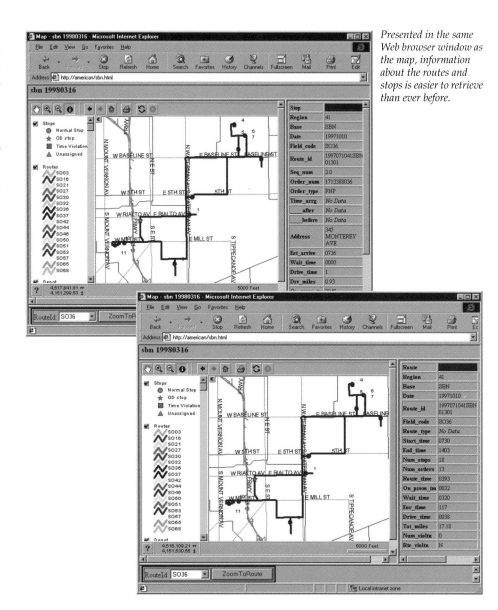

Presented in the same Web browser window as the map, information about the routes and stops is easier to retrieve than ever before.

Map output

In the future, route maps may be automatically printed and provided to the technicians.

Since the routes for a particular region differ considerably from day to day, as the maps at the right show, automation of the process has made everyone's lives much easier.

Feedback from the trenches

To date, there is generally good acceptance of the GRID system by the region supervisors and field service technicians. SoCalGas feels that the GRID system will provide the following benefits: the ability to schedule more service orders per day, and the ability to improve customer satisfaction by meeting service order time arrangements.

And in addition to the improvements in customer service, management will have access through the intranet to a useful tool for planning and monitoring field service operations.

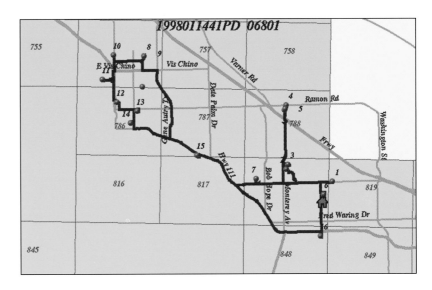

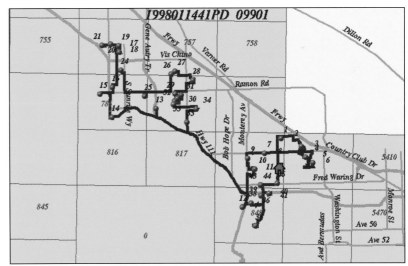

These two maps show the difference in routes that a day makes. Given two different sets of stops, the automated routing system returns two route paths that differ significantly.

Acknowledgments

Thanks to Gil Muramatsu and Julie Wunderlich of Southern California Gas Company, and to Jim McKinny and Ming Zhao of ESRI.

Southern California Gas Company's Web site is at www.socalgas.com.

Southern California Gas Company

Chapter 10

Highway management information systems

Roads and highways are intrinsically geographic. They cover specific parts of the earth's surface and connect physical locations to one another. In addition, many facets about each segment of a road are known or can be measured: what it's made of, when its potholes were last repaired, how high above the river that bridge is, how many cars will pass a given point in the next hour. In light of this, it's no surprise that transportation departments were among the earliest to manage and disseminate geographic data.

In this chapter, you'll see examples of Internet mapping applications developed by the Department of Transportation in California, a state with more cars, trucks, and assorted motor vehicles than most developed nations.

On the road again

California's Department of Transportation, or Caltrans, manages the nation's busiest state highway system.

With over 15,000 miles of freeways, highways, and roads under its jurisdiction, Caltrans relies on the latest digital technology to help manage its spaghetti empire. Keeping these transportation corridors open and uncongested is no small challenge, considering that the majority of California's thirty million residents use some part of the system on any given day. While GIS has long been a part of Caltrans' technology arsenal, only recently has the Internet begun to be used for providing access to vital geographic information.

Californians depend on their highway system to keep the economy rolling; Caltrans depends on GIS and the Internet to keep the information flowing.

Stephen P. Teale Data Center

The Stephen P. Teale Data Center is a government agency that acts as the State of California's technology consultant. Not surprisingly, Caltrans is one of Teale's most active clients.

Teale provides its customers a variety of information technology that they can use without making a large investment in hardware, software, and technical expertise themselves.

Teale's GIS Technology Center includes a well-maintained and continually updated library of geographic information. This library includes detailed information about roads, hydrography, railroads, vegetation, land ownership, public land survey, census, air basins, administrative and legislative boundaries, national wetlands inventory, terrain, and more. This GIS library, available at the county or state level, serves as the basis for the prototype GIS applications featured in this chapter.

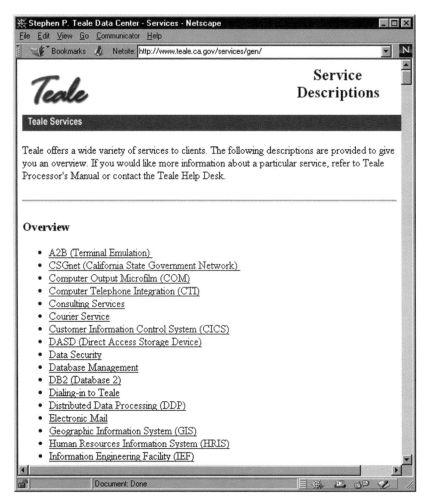

The Stephen P. Teale Data Center helps California state agencies meet their business objectives by providing a variety of technological services and data.

Caltrans Executive Information System

Like many public agencies that use spatial data, Caltrans had built up a large database that was accessible only to a few GIS professionals in its organization.

In an effort to better use this valuable data, it teamed with the GIS people at Teale and created a prototype called the Caltrans Executive Information System— a set of Web-based mapping applications tailored to address the most common functional areas within Caltrans: road and bridge maintenance, traffic operations, and environmental impact analysis.

Once feedback from the prototype users has been evaluated, Caltrans plans to implement this type of system throughout the entire organization. The system needs to be easy enough for nontechnical managers to use, but powerful enough to give technical specialists the functionality and data access they need.

The gateway page shown at the right allows users to navigate to the various modules of the application. A system of user names and passwords lets system administrators establish appropriate areas and levels of access for different employees, based on their job descriptions.

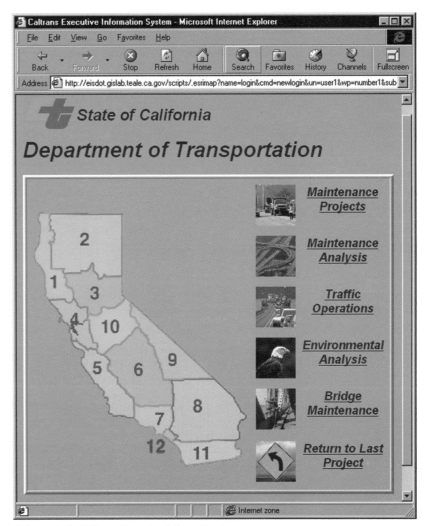

Gateway to the Caltrans Executive Information System.

The user interface

Clicking on the Maintenance Analysis link on the gateway page brings up the map-based interface seen here. The interface shows all the highways that fall under Caltrans jurisdiction, and provides a set of tools for panning and zooming. A user who already knows the location of a particular section of road can navigate the map simply by typing the name of a city or county.

The user can also query the system according to known facts about the maintenance projects. For example, a manager in northern California could ask to see all of the projects in her region with a value of over one million dollars.

Once the map is zoomed in close enough to individual road sections, the user can point to a feature to identify it and bring up detailed maintenance information. The amount and nature of information available to a given user is determined by the permissions held by that user name.

The beauty of the system is that the same interface works for all users and all levels of data they might access. So a bridge engineer can pull up engineering drawings for an overpass, while a landscape supervisor can get the latest tree-trimming report.

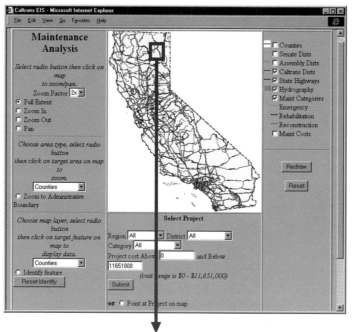

Caltrans road maintenance officials can use this GIS interface to keep tabs on various projects.

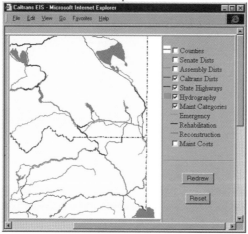

Traffic operations

Traffic operations specialists at Caltrans monitor traffic volume through vehicle counters embedded in roadways. The data provides crucial information used for everything from planning where to designate car pool lanes to when to fix potholes (much work goes on in the middle of the night in urban areas).

The traffic operations interface has the same navigation options as the Maintenance Analysis screen, but provides some new query tools and legend controls.

So instead of selecting stretches of roadway according to maintenance costs, the traffic operators can find the busiest stretch of freeway, or all the freeways with a 70-mile-per-hour speed limit. (The bright red section of highway seen on this map, for example, was highlighted by querying the system for volumes of more than 325,000 vehicles per day.)

The map legend is flexible. In this case, the highways around Los Angeles have been color coded according to specific traffic volumes entered by the user.

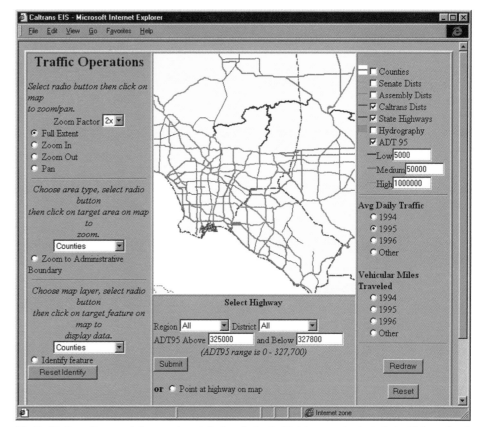

The Traffic Operations module presents an interface similar to Maintenance Analysis, but with legend and query windows specific to the tasks of the traffic operations worker.

Environmental analysis

With highways running through some of the most scenic and environmentally fragile lands in the state, Caltrans has a responsibility to make sure that building and maintaining its roads won't harm nature.

For example, a highway planner charged with resurfacing a stretch of road in the Sierra Nevada Mountains might pull up a detailed map and see that an endangered species of fern is native to the area. As she writes up the work order, she alerts the project manager so that work crews can take care not to uproot any of this sensitive plant.

The concept of the prototype has been well received. Before the end of the decade, Caltrans hopes to take the necessary steps to provide everyone in its organization with access to the system.

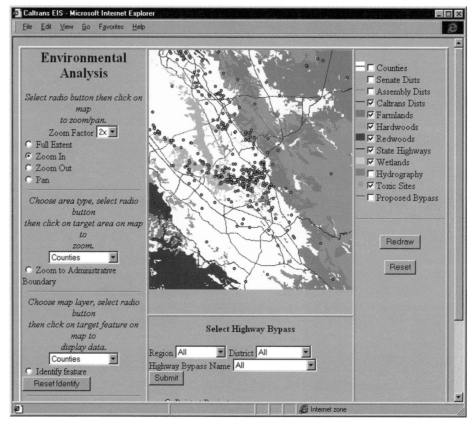

The Environmental Analysis screen allows Caltrans construction and maintenance planners to investigate issues that affect the environment.

Acknowledgments

Thanks to Randy Mori of the Stephen P. Teale Data Center and Diane Pierzinski of Caltrans.

STEPHEN P. TEALE DATA CENTER

Caltrans

Chapter 11

●●●●● Internet yellow pages

Phone companies around the globe spend millions of dollars printing and distributing massive paper directories that are almost immediately out of date. The costs of paper, printing, and distribution coupled with the rising use of the Internet have created an environment in which the incentive to publish online is huge. And sure enough, some of the earliest Web-based GIS applications were Internet yellow pages.

In this chapter, you'll see how the Swedish phone company has used GIS to make its Web-based yellow pages much more useful and interesting than the printed books, and created one of the busiest Web sites in Scandinavia in the process.

Sweden online

Telia (Stockholm, Sweden), owned by the Swedish government and employing more than thirty thousand people, is the dominant force in the Swedish telecommunications market.

Telia not only controls most of Sweden's telecommunications infrastructure (the fixed network, the cellular network, and the cable television network), it also develops cutting-edge Internet applications.

The Swedish Internet Yellow Pages offers round-the-clock access to the most current information available on Swedish businesses, with the added benefit of delivering the information through an interactive map.

Stockholm, Sweden, one of the world's most technologically advanced and progressive telecommunications markets, is the headquarters of Telia.

Yellow pages and more

The site builders thought it important that the interface look like the old paper books. By including its advertisers in the Internet version at no extra cost, Telia can deliver an online version that's as complete as its paper counterpart.

But they also realized they had an opportunity to deliver more data than could ever be contained in a bound volume. This was what would bring people to the Internet, and eventually convince them to abandon the books for good.

The designers also acknowledged the global nature of the Internet by offering two versions of the Web site: one with a Swedish-language interface, and one with an interface in English. This chapter looks at examples from the English-language version.

With a Swedish-language interface and another in English, the Swedish Internet Yellow Pages has become among the most-visited of all European Web sites.

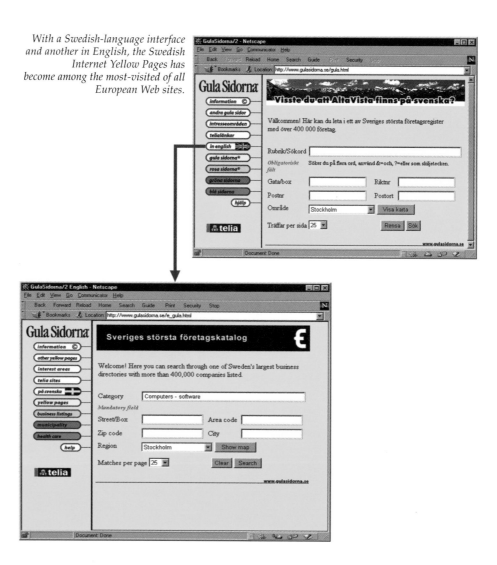

A simple interface

The way the user searches for information mimics the familiar ways of using the paper book, at least at first.

You start by typing in a subject category (like *Computers - software*), or by picking one from an alphabetical list. You can also narrow the search geographically by choosing a region (Stockholm, in this example), postal code, or even street address. Because the database covers all of Sweden, specifying a certain geographic region can limit the results considerably.

The system returns a list of subcategories showing the number of businesses in each. Clicking on *Computer - consultants* brings up a list of the 520 computer consultants in Stockholm.

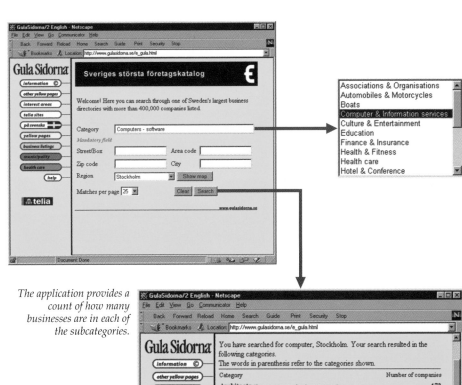

The application provides a count of how many businesses are in each of the subcategories.

A results list

At this point, you're looking at a list of businesses, sorted alphabetically. Under the name, address, and telephone number is a one-sentence description of the business. To the right, a set of green symbols indicates the availability of more detailed information (the big "i"), an Internet presence (the "website" and "e-mail" buttons), or an interactive map (the "map" button). At the time of this writing, businesses must pay an extra premium to have the mapping function included with their listing.

Clicking on the large "i" gives the user a description of the company's business. This page can be as lengthy as the business wants. To make sure that the data is as up-to-date and complete as possible, Telia gives businesses four chances a year to update their information.

You've already received more information than could be gotten from the old-fashioned yellow pages, but this is only the beginning.

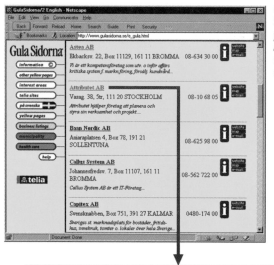

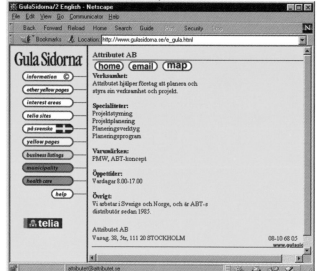

Clicking on the name of the company brings up a description of it. At this point, the information is in Swedish only, although automated language translators may someday make even this part of the information bilingual.

More and more

Clicking on the map button brings up a detailed street map of the area of Stockholm where the business is situated, with a star marking its exact location. Moreover, the map is not static. Because it's created on the fly from a GIS database, it includes controls for panning and zooming that allow you to get closer or to scroll over to another part of the city to find your way to the business from where you are.

The system also includes a link to the company's own home page or e-mail address (if it has one).

In short, the system delivers much more information, and keeps it more up-to-date, than is possible with paper books.

This is where the Swedish Internet Yellow Pages becomes far more useful than its paper predecessor.

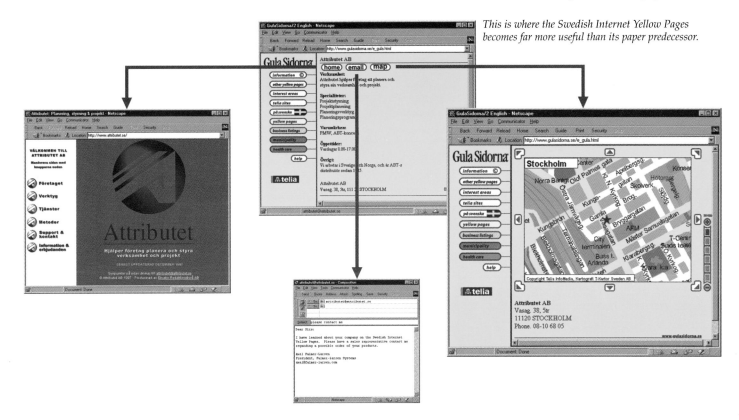

System configuration

The Swedish Internet Yellow Pages application is served with the Oracle Webserver running on a UNIX-based Sun Microsystems workstation. All of the attribute data is stored in an Oracle database, while the map data is stored in a separate Oracle database running ESRI's Spatial Database Engine (SDE) spatial data access engine.

The mapping component of the application is built with MapObjects and Delphi™ software and runs on a Microsoft Windows NT server.

The system provides each user with map data on the fly. Data output from MapObjects software is served as GIF images. All images are temporarily stored on a disk. The least frequently used images are then erased while those used most often are cached for faster access by other users.

As of spring 1998, the system processes more than 500,000 requests per month, and the level of usage is increasing at 5 to 10 percent every month. Even if the growth continues at this rate, the scalable nature of the system ensures that Telia will be able to deliver responses to the requestor in under five seconds.

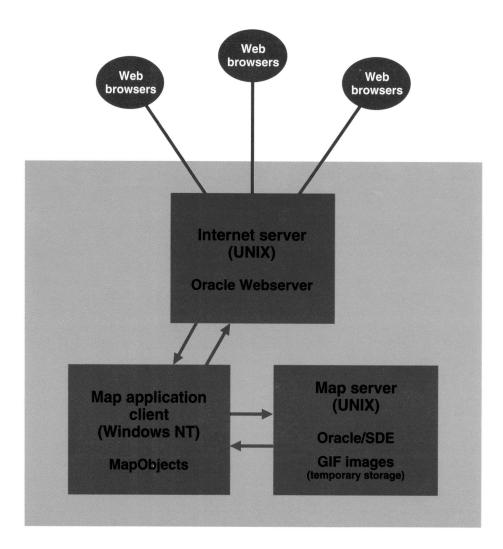

Acknowledgments

Thanks to Susann Nilsson of Telia
InfoMedia Respons AB and Anki Svardby
of T-Kartor, Sweden.

The English-interface version of this Web
site is located at www.gulasidorna.se/
e_gula.html.

Chapter 12

•••••• S c i e n t i f i c   d a t a   p u b l i s h i n g

Nowadays, much of what moves or changes in time and in space can be measured. But however precise or sophisticated the instruments, the data is of limited value if it can't be shared or used in a standard environment. Large geoscience organizations have increasingly seen the need for tools that allow them to share and publish geospatial data in a standard desktop environment.

In this chapter, you'll see some desktop applications developed by America's largest earth science and mapping agency, whose innovative GIS data publishing has helped to usher in an era of increased cooperation and data sharing among federal agencies that manage natural resources.

Science for a changing world

The U.S. Geological Survey (USGS) was established in 1879, principally to classify the public lands of the West according to the presence of gold, silver, copper, and other minerals. Subsequent legislation expanded the Survey's role to include investigating the nation's water supplies and publishing topographic maps.

Though still involved in mineral exploration, today's USGS also collects mountains of geospatial data and performs extensive research on environmental issues far beyond its historical mining purview. With other federal agencies and the public increasingly requesting access to this information, the USGS in conjunction with ESRI has developed a GIS application internally referred to as GeoExplorer.

While the USGS of old studied the formation and location of mineral deposits, today's USGS is as likely to be determining the environmental impact of mines such as this.

The Livengood GeoExplorer

The GeoExplorer concept actually made its debut offline, in a CD–ROM known as the Livengood GeoExplorer. This application distributed geoscience and related base data for the Livengood, Alaska, region where gold exploration is ongoing.

Using ESRI's MapObjects component-based GIS technology, developers constructed the application rapidly by working with reusable building blocks, or components, that each have specific mapping functionality. For the USGS team, this meant they could develop their application once using standard Windows[®] development methods, and then easily modify it for other geographic areas or for different application purposes (like the Internet version of the GeoExplorer you'll see next).

The first thing a user sees is an overview of Alaska that puts the study area in context and links to a close-up of the Livengood region. A series of hierarchically structured views provides easy access to different kinds of data. Intuitive tools control navigation. By selecting the "Mineral Resource Potential" view, the user can access detailed data that estimates the potential for gold and other minerals. This data can be displayed, queried, and plotted on a map.

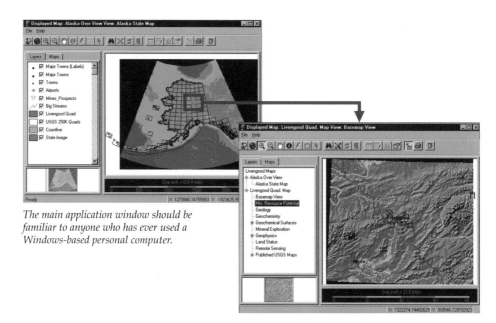

The main application window should be familiar to anyone who has ever used a Windows-based personal computer.

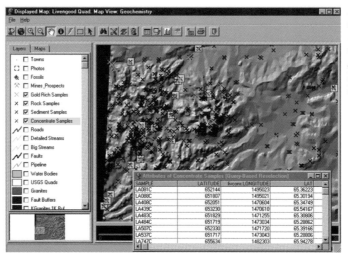

In this graphic, the system's been queried to display gold concentrations greater than 100 parts per billion (shown in yellow squares).

The Internet GeoExplorer

Based on the success of the Livengood project, the USGS next decided to develop a prototype called the Montana GeoEnvironmental Explorer with an Internet component that allows online viewing, sharing, and downloading of data. The project looked specifically at abandoned mines in Montana to see how past mining is affecting the surrounding environment.

The Montana GeoExplorer came about because scientists in different agencies and organizations needed a common platform to share and make available a large quantity of scientific data. Information technology managers responsible for building the Montana application chose the GeoExplorer approach in a Web environment because of the rapid development time it promised, the reusability of components, and the ability to quickly deploy a Web-based GIS application.

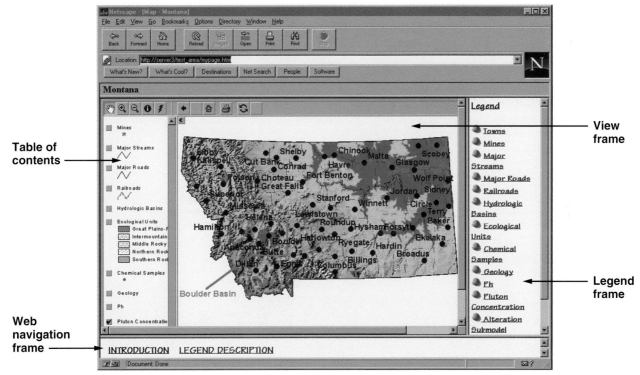

After logging onto the system, a user of the Montana GeoExplorer is presented with an overview map of Montana and a set of frames that contain additional controls.

The legend frame

What makes the Web a web is its ability to connect any given page to many other sources of information located at different sites. The GeoExplorer exploits this functionality by using HTML frames to present additional information without making users leave the application.

The example seen here shows a map of major towns in Montana in relation to pluton concentrations. (A pluton is a granitic rock formation that may have high concentrations of metallic minerals.) To learn more about the pluton submodel, the user clicks on the link in the legend frame. The resulting page explains the pluton submodel, how the data was collected, and how to read the symbology.

Frames can be resized within the browser window. For instance, the Pluton Submodel frame can be widened to make the text more readable at a glance.

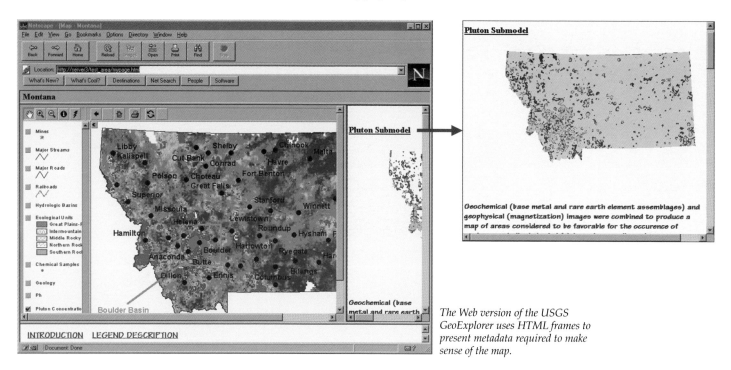

The Web version of the USGS GeoExplorer uses HTML frames to present metadata required to make sense of the map.

The RDBMS connection

The beauty of GIS on the Web is that a single feature on a GIS map can be linked, or related, to any number of external tables through an identifying code; GeoExplorer does just that. In the language of the relational database management system (RDBMS), this is referred to as a one-to-many relationship.

In the example seen here, the map layers for major roads and chemical samples are displayed. The columns in the frame at the right show the tabular results generated by pointing at three individual features with the Identify tool. This data is stored in a Microsoft Access database and is retrieved by the application.

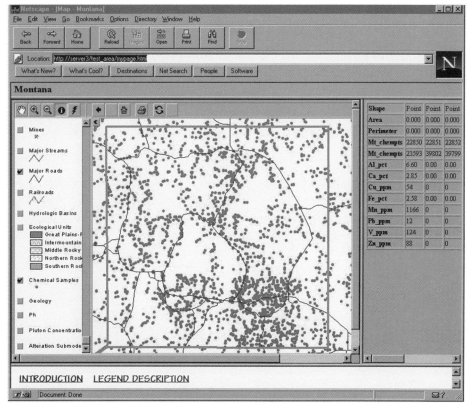

This map shows the locations where chemical samples were taken. By using the Identify tool, the user can access the database information about each sample.

Multimedia hotlinking

Another function USGS wanted was the ability to link map views to other multimedia content like still images, movie clips, and even sound files.

In this example, hundreds of mines are displayed on a map of watersheds. Watersheds are particularly important in this region, as fish habitat within the watershed is affected by the concentration of metals leaching into it.

Many of the point features representing the mines are linked to photographs. When the user clicks on a particular point, a photograph of the site is displayed in a resizable frame at the right side of the application window.

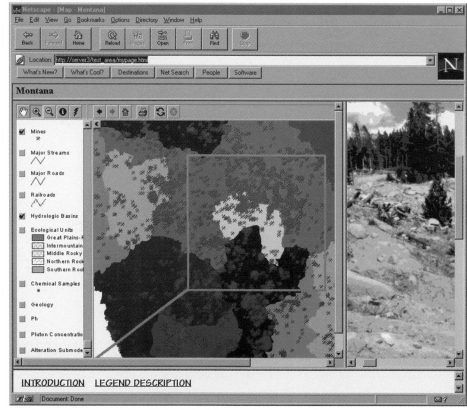

In this example, a photo of a heavily leached mining area is shown in relation to watersheds in the study area.

Downloading data

The system architects knew that while viewing spatial data online was a necessary and important aspect of the GeoExplorer project, it wasn't enough in and of itself. They also wanted to create a means by which people could put USGS data on their own computers for their own projects.

To do this, they built links into the system that allow users to download the data being viewed in the format of their choice.

For example, a reporter writing a news story on mine reclamation in Montana might download a map as a TIFF image file that could be used in a word-processing or page layout program. A scientist with GIS software and experience might download a shapefile (.shp) or an ESRI export file (.e00).

The program has been so well received that the USGS now plans to publish much more of its information in this way.

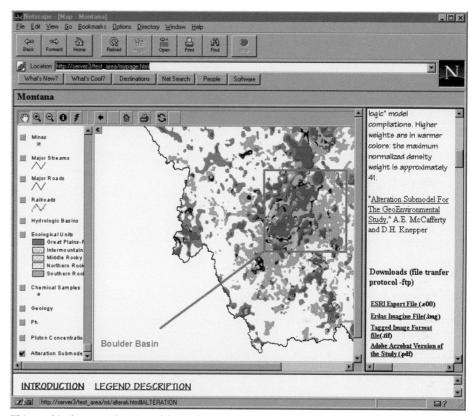

This graphic shows another view of the geochemical makeup of western Montana and the links by which users can download data for their own purposes.

The ongoing benefits

The first and most obvious benefit of the GeoExplorer is that it allows the USGS to distribute the vital work of its geologists and geoscientists to a much wider audience than ever before. But, as so often happens with new technology, there have been unexpected benefits as well.

In this case, the project attracted the attention of other federal agencies interested in the same issues and helped to create an environment that promotes data sharing. Suddenly, agencies that once had very little interaction are cooperating to help tackle the very real and serious environmental problems faced by scientists nationwide.

Acknowledgments

Thanks to Charlie Barnwell of ESRI–Alaska and Linda Gundersen of the United States Geological Survey, Mineral Resources Program.

Chapter 13

Maps and data servers

Internet technology has evolved so rapidly that everyday Web users simply take for granted the existence of massive, sophisticated databases of movie reviews or books for sale. Similarly (though not perhaps to the same degree), they have also come to expect sophisticated mapping applications. In many cases, they don't even think about the fact that they're retrieving spatially referenced information from huge databases and creating maps on the fly.

In this chapter, you'll see a new type of Web site where people are doing everything from obtaining detailed street files of their neighborhoods, to creating maps of Scandinavian unemployment rates to comparing FBI crime statistics from major U.S. cities.

ArcData Online

As the world leader in GIS software and implementations, ESRI (Environmental Systems Research Institute, Inc., Redlands, California) was an early provider of geographic display and analysis software for the Internet.

ArcData℠ Online is ESRI's Web site offering a wealth of geographically referenced data and analysis tools. So whether you're creating a map of global economic output for a school report, purchasing a detailed street network to plan a direct mail campaign, or showing the grandkids where in Siberia your family originated, ArcData Online is the place to go.

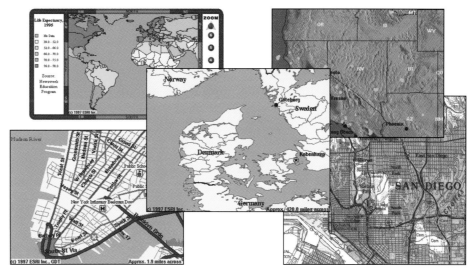

The ArcData Online database contains many kinds of information about the world's people, nations, and environment.

What is ArcData?

The ArcData data set contains geographi-cally referenced information that works with ESRI GIS software. At the ArcData Online Web site, the data is available to download, or to view online as maps that can be organized in an unlimited number of ways. All the data at the site is stored in the industry-standard shapefile (.shp) format.

Shapefiles

The shapefile format is an ideal vehicle for distributing spatial data over the Internet because it uses less disk space than other spatial data formats and thus transmits quickly over computer networks.

Shapefiles can be used to store point, line, and polygon map features. They are linked to attribute information stored in dBASE-format files.

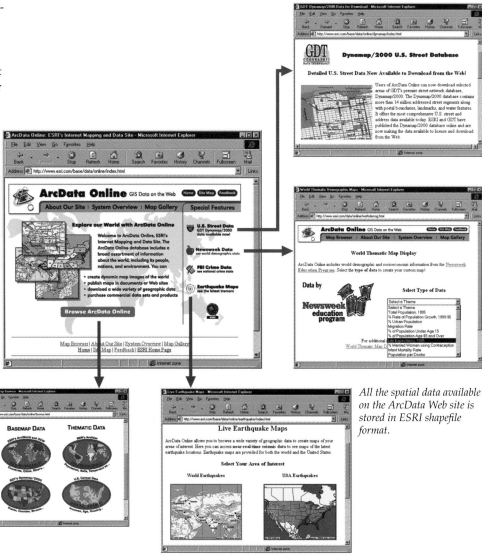

All the spatial data available on the ArcData Web site is stored in ESRI shapefile format.

Two ways to use

To get information from ArcData Online, you can create maps right in your Web browser or you can download data to your own machine.

Using data stored on a server at ESRI in Redlands, California, users can make simple base maps showing political and physical geographies, or thematic maps that represent quantifiable information (like population density) in a geographic context.

Users wanting to save the data for use in their own geographic information system can download it. Using the ArcExplorer GIS data viewer (free, downloadable software from ESRI), they can connect directly to the ArcData Online server to view and select spatial data. And if the free data is not adequate, there's plenty of data to buy, too.

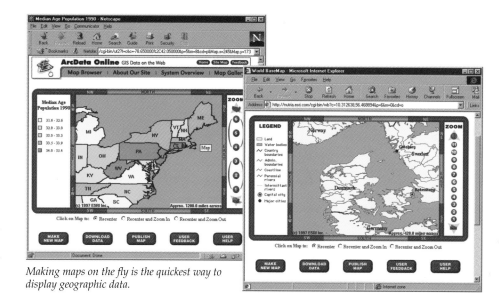

Making maps on the fly is the quickest way to display geographic data.

The ArcExplorer data viewer lets you see what you're getting before you download it.

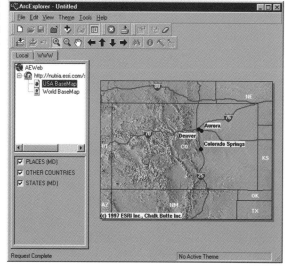

Using maps in other applications

A ninth grader in New Jersey is working on a report about crime-fighting trends for his high school civics class. He wants to include some statistics about auto theft in his report.

He goes to ArcData Online and creates the thematic map at the right depicting car thefts per 100,000 people in the eastern United States. The map shows that fewer car thefts occur in rural inland counties.

Once he has the map composed the way he wants it, he uses the Save Image command on his Web browser to save the map as a bitmap image file that can be inserted into a word-processing document.

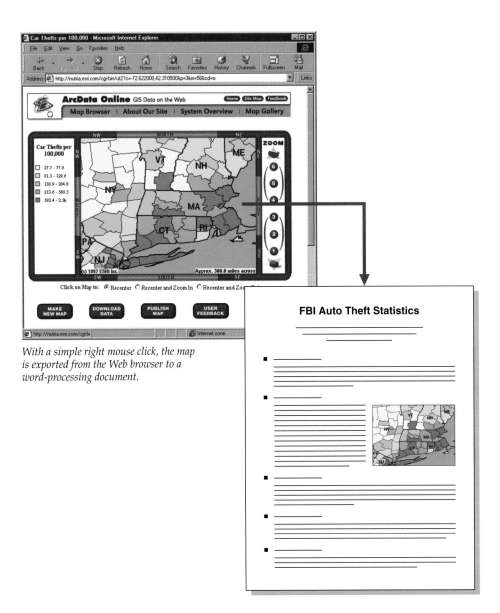

With a simple right mouse click, the map is exported from the Web browser to a word-processing document.

Posting maps on the Web

In the Web era, of course, sometimes even paper documents are superfluous. Posting maps to a Web site is an increasingly popular way to share geographic information with others around the globe.

To promote this innovative notion, the ArcData Online Web site includes a special place where you can post any map that you've created on the system for other people to see.

This type of Web-based geocommunication has tremendous implications both as a learning tool and as a business productivity tool. For example, a group of geography students with the same assignment could all post their work to a common site for comparison and discussion. Or a landscape architecture firm with offices in different cities could post design maps to a common Web server. Architects on opposite sides of the country (or the world, for that matter) could keep up with each other's work.

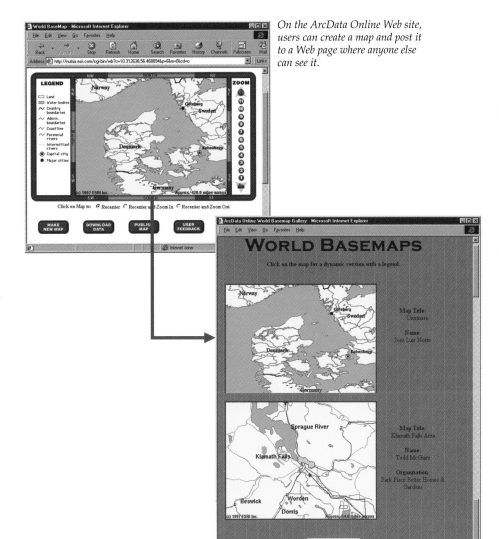

On the ArcData Online Web site, users can create a map and post it to a Web page where anyone else can see it.

Purchasing data online

Pundits have long predicted that Internet commerce will turn out to be the Web's true "killer app," the technology that will bring the masses (or rather, the rest of the masses) to the Internet.

At ArcData Online, Internet commerce has already arrived. People can now go to the site and purchase data from several companies, including the premier U.S. street data provider, Geographic Data Technology (GDT), and Horizons Technology, vendors of Sure!MAPS® RASTER scanned USGS topographic maps.

Buying data online is easy. For example, users needing detailed street data for small geographic areas (like a single ZIP Code) can specify the area they want. They pay $10 to $15 per ZIP Code with a credit card, then download a compressed shapefile that can be used directly in ArcView GIS, ARC/INFO, ArcExplorer, or any other GIS program that reads ESRI shapefiles.

For the consumer, especially someone who just needs a few ZIP Codes' worth of information, this is ideal. There's no waiting, and the data is reasonably priced.

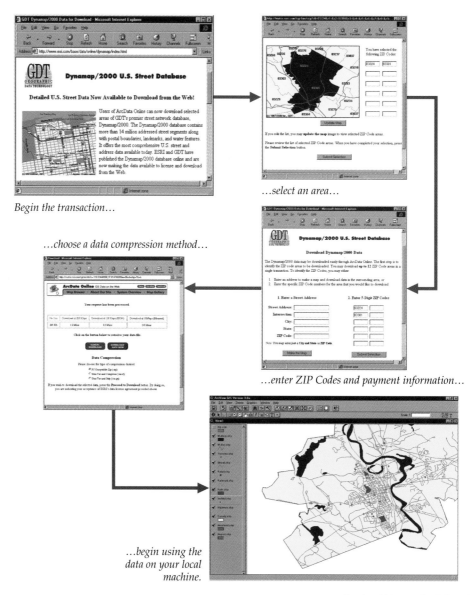

Begin the transaction…

…select an area…

…choose a data compression method…

…enter ZIP Codes and payment information…

…begin using the data on your local machine.

System configuration

The ArcData Online database and mapping system are stored on a Sun Microsystems Enterprise™ 6000 server with eight 200MHz CPUs, 4GB of RAM, and 400GB of disk storage.

This system configuration allows ESRI to support tens of thousands of map requests per day and to generate maps at an average of less than two seconds per request. The system will likely be supporting hundreds of thousands of requests per day in the coming months.

With each request, the system queries data sets that are maintained in ESRI's Spatial Database Engine (SDE) data format for rapid access and retrieval. The results are returned to the user in the form of a map image or data shapefile.

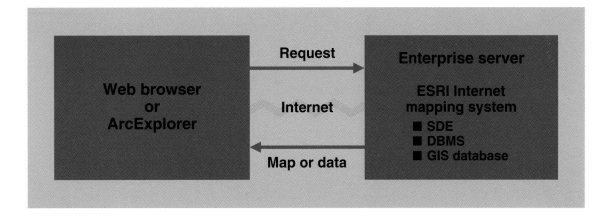

The ESRI Internet mapping story

This description of ESRI's Internet Map Server (IMS) strategy and technologies is a snapshot of the situation at the time of this writing (spring 1998). Developments in Internet and GIS technologies are moving very rapidly, and more products are entering the marketplace every week. ESRI is leading the way in developing and supporting open standards for data and communications protocols. To keep up with developments, bookmark http://www.esri.com/base/products and check there often.

Browser-based versus direct-access applications

An Internet-based GIS application can be delivered through a Web browser or through a dedicated product like ESRI's ArcExplorer GIS data viewer. The choice of which depends on the audience and the required functionality.

In the browser scenario, the user interacts with the application through a standard Web browser. Enabling the interaction on the server side are GIS technologies that may be prepackaged, like ArcView IMS, or custom-built with products like MapObjects and Allaire™ Cold Fusion (an application development system for Web site developers). Applications requiring robust performance may also use Spatial Database Engine software to store and deliver geographic data with Oracle or Informix databases.

In the other scenario, the Internet user actually downloads a GIS application and directly connects to a database through a Web site. The geographic application may be delivered as a Java applet that goes away when no longer in use, or as software that remains installed on the user's computer.

This dedicated-access method is more powerful than a browser-based solution because it allows the user to directly manipulate and retrieve the data underlying the application. When not connected to the Internet, the dedicated-access application can also work on locally stored data.

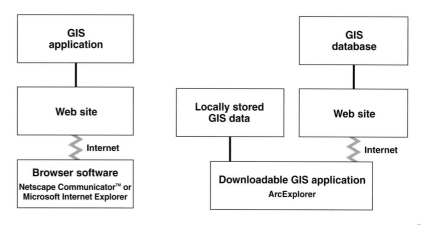

ArcExplorer

ESRI's ArcExplorer data viewer is a direct-access GIS application. It has a small memory footprint, which means it starts quickly and doesn't use much in the way of computing resources.

The ArcExplorer product is really two applications in one: it's both a data viewer and a data retrieval tool.

As a stand-alone data viewer, ArcExplorer software can display and query GIS data in shapefile and ARC/INFO formats. It can also create thematic maps based on user-defined variables and save them in standard image formats.

As a data retrieval tool, the software can access GIS data sites (like www.esri.com/base/data/online), browse the spatial data located there, and initiate a download of the information as GIS data, not as image files.

The ArcExplorer data viewer/retriever can be installed as a stand-alone application (top graphic) or as an ActiveX® plug-in to a Web browser like Netscape Navigator or Microsoft Internet Explorer (bottom graphic).

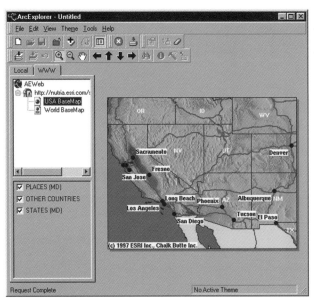

The basic version of the ArcExplorer data viewer/retriever is a stand-alone application that can connect to map-serving sites independently of a Web browser.

The ActiveX version of ArcExplorer software is installed as a plug-in to standard Web browsers and runs inside the browser window.

ArcView Internet Map Server

The easiest way to create a browser-based GIS application is using an off-the-shelf program such as ArcView Internet Map Server (IMS) software. ArcView IMS is an extension to ArcView GIS software that allows you to publish maps on the Web almost as easily as you send a document to a printer.

With ArcView IMS, no programming is required to serve maps on the Internet. With the help of a wizard tool, you automatically create a Web page from a specified ArcView GIS project and deliver a Java applet to the client computer. You then employ controls on the applet to visualize, browse, and query the ArcView GIS maps as if they were running locally, not on the World Wide Web or an intranet.

ArcView IMS works with Windows 95® and Windows NT. ArcView IMS is also available in a UNIX version.

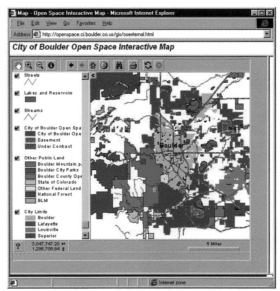

Applications served with ArcView Internet Map Server (like this one from the City of Boulder, Colorado) present Web users with easy-to-understand controls.

MapObjects Internet Map Server

The MapObjects collection of software objects delivers a wide range of GIS tools for map navigation, analysis, and communication in the form of individual components. These components can be embedded in other applications and used with programming languages like Visual Basic and Cold Fusion to add mapping functionality to many different software applications.

One such component is the MapObjects Internet Map Server (IMS), which delivers mapping and GIS over the Internet (or an intranet based on TCP/IP standards).

In a typical MapObjects IMS application, user requests are processed by MapObjects software via a standard Web browser. The results are returned to the client as raw data, as HTML files, or as image data stored in GIF or JPEG format.

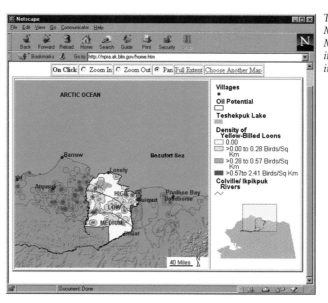

The U.S. Bureau of Land Management uses MapObjects IMS as part of its online environmental impact report.

The locator at Nursing Home INFO uses MapObjects IMS to match addresses and display the results on a map.

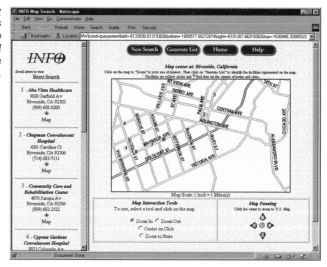

SDE

As online applications become larger (with multimillion-record databases), more popular (with thousands of concurrent users), and more complex (involving, for example, the three-dimensional display of spatial data), Spatial Database Engine (SDE) software will become increasingly important to Internet GIS. It answers these challenges because it allows spatial data to coexist with other types of data in heavy-duty database environments (like Oracle or Informix) that can be scaled up as needed to handle information growth and increasing usage.

The SDE spatial data access engine is important for certain large mapping sites on the Web, like the Telstra Australian white pages seen here.

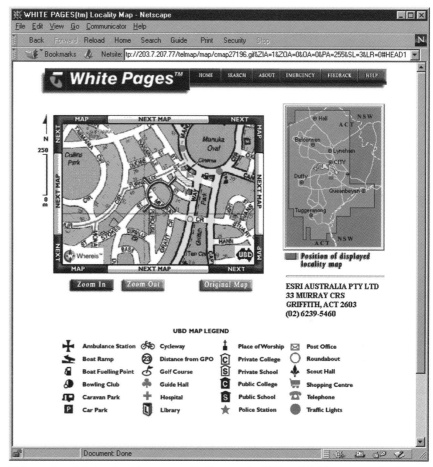

This map-based electronic white pages application uses the SDE spatial data access engine to handle millions of hits monthly, often with thousands of concurrent users.

Future directions

On the client side, the trend is that a higher percentage of people will access geographic information directly with programs like the ArcExplorer data viewer and custom clients, while even more will get on the Web and use standard Web browsers.

On the server side, ESRI is developing a new breed of Internet Map Server technology based on the current MapObjects architecture. The new IMS technology will run across platforms and work with all of ESRI's existing mapping solutions. It's a new type of middleware technology that handles all the network communications between increasingly specialized mapping engines and the map-consuming public.

ESRI took a major step toward creating an industry-standard GIS data model by publishing the shapefile format. This emerging data standard coupled with the technology standards promised by the next generation of IMS will stimulate the ongoing expansion of GIS services on the Internet.

Appendix B

Mapping applications on the Web

This appendix lists some interactive mapping applications on the World Wide Web. The links on this page can be accessed directly online at www.esri.com/esribooks or on the companion CD–ROM. All of the links were checked shortly before this book went to press, but given the dynamic nature of the Web, some sites may not be accessible.

http://www.esri.com/base/data/online

ArcData Online—An extensive online database of geographic data and a mapping engine.

http://www.realtor.com

Realtor.com—Search over one million new and resale homes.

http://www.co.cabarrus.nc.us

Cabarrus County—A county government public-access property ownership and tax records database.

http://mapfinder.nos.noaa.gov

National Ocean Service MapFinder Home Page—A one-stop World Wide Web service that provides direct Internet access to primary NOS imagery and data holdings.

http://www.macavsat.org

Metropolitan Airports Commission Department of Environment Web site—Web-based airport noise and operations monitoring system at the Minneapolis Metropolitan Airports Commission.

http://www.inforain.org

Interrain Pacific INFORAIN Web Site—Bioregional Geographic Information Server for the North American coastal rain forest.

http://www.gulasidorna.se/e_gula.html

GulaSidorna/2 English—Sweden's largest online business directory.

http://icg.fas.harvard.edu/~maps

Harvard University Map Collection—Links to the Massachusetts Electronic Atlas and other Internet GIS resources.

http://gis.ci.ontario.ca.us/gis

City of Ontario, California, Geographic Information Web Server—A parcel search and site locator.

http://gis.mit.edu/projects

Computer Resource Lab at MIT—Links to Internet GIS research projects in progress.

http://godiva.geoserve.com/forms/godiva.htm

Godiva Chocolate—Godiva Chocolatier U.S. store locator.

http://www.nursinghomeinfo.com

Nursing Home INFO—Nationwide Nursing Home Directory. Click on "Find a Nursing Home."

http://openspace.ci.boulder.co.us/gis/osmap.html

City of Boulder Open Space Interactive Map—Public-access GIS site established to promote discussion of open space issues in Boulder, Colorado.

http://poca.osmre.gov

West Virginia Division of Environmental Protection—Create customized maps of environmental issues affecting the state of West Virginia.

http://www.stickmap.com

Seismic Geophysical Exploration Data from @stickmap.com—Commercial data vendor site.

http://www.epa.gov/enviro/html/mod/index.html

U.S. Environmental Protection Agency, Maps On Demand—Interactive mapping applications and a storehouse of environmental data.

http://www.snapper.com/dealers

Snapper Dealer Locator—U.S. sales and service locator designed to help a user find nearest Snapper dealer.

http://192.243.139.248

West Virginia DEP Mapping & Query Interface—An interactive mapping interface that uses a CGI interface to ARC/INFO software to generate maps and query attribute data for the state of West Virginia.

http://www.visa.com

Visa–ATM Locator—Interactive bank and ATM locator.

http://alexandria.sdc.ucsb.edu

The Alexandria Digital Library—Links to significant collections of geospatially referenced information.

http://www.weather.com/weather/maps/index.html

The Weather Channel—Interactive weather-mapping site.

http://www.maxwell.com/caltrans

Southern California Traffic Report—Real-time traffic conditions for Southern California.

http://plue.sedac.ciesin.org/plue/ddviewer

Demographic Data Viewer Home Page—Java-based interactive census data viewer.

http://www.inberkeley2.ci.berkeley.ca.us/crimeinfo

City of Berkeley Crime Information Web site—Interactive crime maps let citizens see where crime is happening in the city.

http://civic-center.ci.sf.ca.us/recpark/neighbor.nsf/neighborhoods

City of San Francisco Parks and Recreation—Neighborhood activities mapping application.

http://wgdb.sdvc.uwyo.edu/misc/home.html

Wyoming Geologic Database—Obtain and analyze geologic and other science-related information about Wyoming.

http://publiguias.cl

Publiguias—Online map-based business directory for Chile.

http://www.landuse.com/mapsforp.htm

Southwestern Colorado Data Center—Maps for People site distributes GIS data over the Internet to rural Coloradans.

http://www.kfwis.state.ky.us/kfwisbeta/kbba/framekb-baopen.htm

Kentucky Breeding Bird Atlas Database—Create maps of the distribution of individual bird species.

http://www.mapsonus.com

Maps On Us—A map, route, and yellow pages service.

http://www.whitepages.com.au

Australian white pages—Online access to eight million residential, business, and government listings.

http://www.kalmar.se/turism/kartor

Kartor over Kalmar—An interactive map of Kalmar, Sweden, is part of the city's extensive tourism Web site.

http://www.erin.gov.au/database/db.html

ERIN Database Gateway—Mapping utilities as part of the Environment Australia Web site.

http://www.gisca.adelaide.edu.au/cgi-bin/eco/ecogis

Ecotourism Interactive GIS—An interactive map designed to plan ecotours.

http://opgis.lst.se/text1.htm

Interactive GIS Application—This Swedish-language application contains examples of air pollution sources and nature reserves in selected areas of Sweden.

http://www.krak.dk/ntsc4_default.htm

KRAK AS—A Danish-language electronic atlas of Denmark.

http://www.pmel.noaa.gov/vents/coax/coax.html

CoAxial Home Page—The VENTS GIS is used for mapping and the integration, display, and management of a wide range of scientific data.

http://epawww.ciesin.org/arc/map-home.html

Great Lakes Map Server—The prototype Great Lakes Map Server allows interactive composition of maps of local areas within the Great Lakes region of the United States.

http://ice.ucdavis.edu:8080/ice_maps

ICE MAPS: Interactive California Environmental Management, Assessment, and Planning System—An interactive environmental information system.

http://www.lib.virginia.edu/gic

University of Virginia Library Geographic Information Center—Links to several interactive mapping programs covering Virginia.

http://www.unh-eos-explorer.sr.unh.edu

UNH EOS Explorer—Prototype Java application features data from Brazil's Legal Amazon region and contains a total of thirty-seven themes.

http://spp-www.cdf.ca.gov/mapmaker

California Department of Forestry and Fire Protection Map Making Facility—Demonstrates some simple map production capabilities over the Internet.

http://commnt2.ci.high-point.nc.us/statlas.html

High Point, North Carolina, GIS—Interactive street locator database.

http://www.sangis.org

SanGIS: San Diego Geographic Information Source—The SanGIS Interactive Mapping page offers maps of San Diego County from regional to street level.

http://www.metro-dade.com/servicesatoz.htm

Miami-Dade County Services A to Z—Map-based county government service locator.

http://www.kennebunk.maine.org/mapserver/home.html

Town of Kennebunk ~ Mapserver Index—Links to several interactive street, parcel, and other maps.

http://www.gis.umn.edu/snf/info/brochures/maps.html

Superior National Forest Map—Interactive map server.

http://www.ramaker.com/gis/pds/pdsmapfrm.htm

Village of Prairie du Sac, Wisconsin—Interactive GIS Web site where citizens can access local GIS data online.

http://www.fmri.usf.edu/surf

Florida Marine Research Institute—Interactive mapping application for browsing the conditions and vulnerability of any of the 2,111 watersheds within the continental United States.

http://www.compass.ie/epa/system.html

Environmental Protection Agency, Ireland—Interactive mapping system on water quality.

http://www.maproom.psu.edu

Penn State University Libraries: Maps and Data Center—Links to interactive mapping applications like Pennsylvania Statistics by County and the Digital Chart of the World.

http://viva.lib.virginia.edu/gic/spatial/tiger.browse.html

University of Virginia Library Geographic Information Center—The Virginia County Interactive Mapper makes customized maps of every Virginia city and county.

http://crusty.er.usgs.gov:80/mapit

U.S. Geological Survey Map-It—Form-based map generator uses latitude/longitude coordinates to create local maps.

http://www.cast.uark.edu/products/MAPPER

University of Arkansas—Arkansas Interactive Mapper.

Additional resources

Here are some excellent resources to help expand your knowledge of GIS:

- *Getting to Know ArcView GIS* from ESRI is the definitive how-to text about the popular desktop GIS application. Order it and other ESRI Press titles online at *www.esri.com/base/store*.

- *GIS-L* and *ArcView-L* are Internet discussion groups where users answer each other's questions and discuss GIS issues.

- *1-800-GIS-XPRT (447-9778)* is ESRI's toll-free information line that works from anywhere in the United States. Telephone *909-793-2853* to reach ESRI from anywhere else in the world.

- The *ArcData Catalog* is a comprehensive description of ESRI-software-compatible data.

- *User guides and online documentation* included with ESRI Internet Map Server products will answer the toughest questions.

- *GIS World* is an international magazine focusing on GIS technology and applications. For information, contact *GIS World,* Fort Collins, Colorado.

- *www.esri.com* is the starting place for accessing all of ESRI's Internet resources.

- To *contact the author* directly, send e-mail to *charder@esri.com*. To participate in a discussion forum related to this book, link to the ESRI Press book conferences at *www.esri.com/esribooks*.

Glossary

ActiveX A set of Microsoft technologies that enables software components to interact with one another in a networked environment.

applet A small Java program that runs within a Web page.

ARC/INFO A GIS software package from ESRI that runs on UNIX workstations and Windows NT. Map files created with ARC/INFO software may be used in ArcView GIS projects.

ArcView Internet Map Server An ArcView GIS extension that supports live mapping and GIS applications on the World Wide Web.

ArcView Spatial Analyst An ArcView GIS extension that supports spatial and statistical analysis of raster data and the integrated use of raster and vector data.

attribute A piece of information describing a map feature. The attributes of a ZIP Code, for example, might include its area, population, and average per capita income. Attribute data is one of the two main types of data in a GIS (the other being spatial data).

browser Client software used to access resources on the Web.

CAD Computer-assisted drafting program, sometimes used for making maps.

CGI (Common Gateway Interface) Common Gateway Interface. An interface-creation scripting program that allows on-the-fly creation of WWW pages based on information from buttons, check boxes, text input, and so on.

client/server architecture A common framework for distributing applications such as GIS on the Internet. Information and applications are stored on one or more servers, which can be accessed by clients connected to the Internet.

dBASE file A file format native to dBASE data management software. ArcView GIS software can read, create, and export tables in dBASE format.

demographics The statistical characteristics of a population (for example, income, education, and home ownership).

desktop GIS A geographic information system, such as ArcView GIS software, that runs on a personal computer.

digital elevation model A topographic surface arranged in a data file as a set of x,y,z coordinates where *z* equals elevation.

digitizing The process of electronically tracing features on a paper map to convert them to features in a digital map file. Accomplished with a device called a *digitizing tablet*.

feature A map representation of a geographic object. Store sites, customer locations, streets, census tracts, and ZIP Codes are examples of map features. Features are drawn in ArcView GIS software as points, lines, and polygons.

frames An extension to HTML that allows the Web page designer to divide the main window of a Web browser into separate panels.

geocoding	The process of converting location data stored as records (for instance, a database of customer addresses) into accurately placed features in a map file. ArcView GIS software has built-in geocoding capabilities.
geographic information system (GIS)	A configuration of computer hardware and software that stores, displays, and analyzes geographic data.
GIF	Graphical Interchange Format. The most common file format for displaying images on the Internet. Identified by the .gif extension.
HTML	HyperText Markup Language. The programming language in which World Wide Web documents are written.
HTTP	HyperText Transfer Protocol. The common protocol used to transmit documents on the World Wide Web.
image data	One of the three types of spatial data in a GIS (the others being raster and vector data). Photographs taken from satellites and airplanes are examples of image data.
Internet	A decentralized computer network linking tens of thousands of smaller networks and accessed by more than thirty million users worldwide. Users connected to the Internet can send and receive e-mail, download files, view multimedia content on the World Wide Web, and run software applications stored on remote computers.
intranet	A computer network with restricted access (as, for example, within a company) that uses standard Internet protocols like HTML and HTTP.
IP address	Every machine on the Internet has a unique IP number. If a machine does not have an IP number, it is not really on the Internet.

Java   An object-oriented programming language for developing Internet applications. Java is platform-independent, which means that its programs run on different operating systems (UNIX, Windows, Macintosh, and so on).

JPEG   Joint Photographic Experts Group. The best file format for storing and displaying photographs on the Internet. Reduces file size by up to twenty times and identified by the .jpg extension.

layer   A set of related map features and attributes, stored as a unique file in a geographic database. A GIS can display multiple layers (for instance, counties, roads, and hamburger stands) at the same time.

metadata   A definition or description of data.

NetEngine   A programmer's library for network modeling, pathfinding, and tracing of network topology.

plug-in   Software that automatically works in a Web browser when particular types of files are encountered.

protocol   A language by which two computers communicate. Common Internet protocols include HTTP and TCP/IP.

raster data   One of the three types of spatial data in a GIS (the others being image and vector data). Raster data represents geographic space as a matrix of cells; map features are defined by numeric values assigned to the cells.

remote sensing   The acquisition of data from a distance, such as by satellite imagery or aerial photography.

shapefile   A file format developed by ESRI for storing the location, shape, and attribute information of geographic features.

spatial analysis   The determination of the spatial relationships between geographic objects, such as the distance between them or the extent to which they overlap.

spatial data   One of the two main types of data in a GIS (the other being attribute data). Spatial data represents the shape, location, or appearance of geographic objects. It can be in vector, raster, or image format.

symbol   A particular graphic element or icon (defined by some combination of shape, size, color, angle, outline, and fill pattern) used to draw a map feature. An airport, for example, might be represented by an icon of a blue airplane. ArcView GIS software comes with hundreds of symbols to choose from; additional symbols can be created from fonts or imported from images.

symbology   The aspect of map design dealing with the choice of symbols, colors, and text fonts.

TCP/IP   Transmission Control Protocol/Internet Protocol. The group of protocols that defines the Internet. Originally created for the UNIX operating system, TCP/IP software is now usable for every major computer operating system. To be truly on the Internet, a computer must have TCP/IP software.

thematic map   A map that symbolizes features according to a particular attribute. A map displaying businesses as dots of different sizes according to number of employees, and a map displaying census tracts in different colors according to median household income, are examples.

TIGER The U.S. Census Bureau's digital geographic database. (TIGER is an acronym for Topographically Integrated Geographic Encoding and Referencing.) The TIGER database contains complete coverage of the United States and its territories. It defines the location and relationship of streets, rivers, railroads, and other features to each other and to the numerous geographic entities (such as census tracts) for which the Census Bureau tabulates data.

URL Uniform Resource Locator. The address for a site on the World Wide Web, like http://www.esri.com.

vector data One of the three types of spatial data in a GIS (the others being image and raster data). Vector data represents geographic objects as points, lines, or polygons.

VRML Virtual Reality Modeling Language. A standard data mode used to describe three-dimensional environments.

World Wide Web A client/server system for distributing and accessing multimedia documents on the Internet. Documents on the World Wide Web are formatted in a special language called HTML (HyperText Markup Language) that supports links to other documents.